Penguin Masterstudies

Doctor Faustus

GW00792429

Michael Mangan is Lecturer in English at Sheffield University.

Penguin Masterstudies
Advisory Editors:
Stephen Coote and Bryan Loughrey

Christopher Marlowe

Doctor Faustus

Michael Mangan

Penguin Books

To Zara and Rachael

Penguin Books Ltd, Harmondsworth, Middlesex, England
Viking Penguin Inc., 40 West 23rd Street, New York, New York 10010, U.S.A.
Penguin Books Australia Ltd, Ringwood, Victoria, Australia
Penguin Books Canada Ltd, 2801 John Street, Markham, Ontario, Canada L3R 1B4
Penguin Books (N.Z.) Ltd, 182–190 Wairau Road, Auckland 10, New Zealand

First published 1987

Made and printed in Great Britain by
Richard Clay Ltd, Bungay, Suffolk
Filmset in 9/11pt Monophoto Times

Acknowledgements

In preparing this volume, I have had help and support from many people and institutions. In particular, I would like to thank The Fulbright Commission, the British Academy, the University of Sheffield and the University of Maryland. The staff at the Folger Shakespeare Library, Washington DC, were unfailingly helpful and made the research a pleasure. Individually, I would like to extend thanks to students and colleagues, both past and present, at the Universities of Sheffield and Maryland, and most especially to Michael Hattaway, Roma Gill, Brian Morris, Philip Roberts, Marion Trousdale, Ted Leinwand and Neil and RoseAnn Fraistat; also to Stephen Coote, Bryan Loughrey and Zara Mangan. All of these, whether knowingly or not, helped to make the writing of this book a more pleasurable and easier task. To none of them, of course, should any of the remaining faults be attributed.

Michael Mangan
Washington DC, 1986

Contents

Marlowe's Life: Some Important Dates

1564

Christopher Marlowe born in Canterbury. The baptismal entry in the parish church of St George the Martyr reads, 'The 26th day of ffebruary was Christened Christopher the sonne of John Marlow.' A February birthday (he was probably christened very shortly after birth; three days seems to have been the norm) would make Marlowe just two months older than his great contemporary, William Shakespeare. Shakespeare's father, also called John, made gloves; John Marlowe made shoes. Both John Marlowe and John Shakespeare seem to have originally been prosperous men who performed public duties in their respective small provincial towns, later falling on comparatively hard times. The similarity between the very early backgrounds of the two playwrights is striking, but their paths begin to diverge when we consider their respective educations.

1579

Marlowe obtains scholarship to the King's School, Canterbury. Shakespeare also went to a 'King's School' – more precisely, the King's New School at Stratford-upon-Avon. Although in all likelihood it was better than the majority of rural grammar schools, it pales into insignificance when compared with Marlowe's King's School in Canterbury. The most ancient in England, Marlowe's school, primarily dedicated to the education of the sons of gentlemen, also provided scholarships for the education of 'fifty poor boys'. Marlowe, who would have received an education up to the age of fourteen at one of the small local schools of Canterbury, was awarded one of these scholarships in January 1579 – thereby allowing the cobbler's son access to the routes towards power.

1580

Marlowe obtains scholarship to Corpus Christi College, Cambridge. Corpus Christi's three Archbishop Parker Scholarships each provided for an endowment of £3 6s 8d per year, and one of them was reserved for a native of Canterbury who was a scholar of the King's School.

Marlowe was awarded the scholarship in 1580 – another vital step in his career. Oxford and Cambridge were the intellectual centres of the country and, since they were essentially theological institutions, they were closely enmeshed in the power structures of the Elizabethan Church. Marlowe's scholarship stipend, which was to last for the full six years of the curriculum, was intended to support him in the study of divinity, which would be followed, in theory, by his taking Holy Orders.

1584

Marlowe becomes Bachelor of Arts. The first stage of the Cambridge education was also usually the time when a student made up his mind concerning a career in the Church. There is evidence to suggest that after 1584 Marlowe, while still pursuing his studies at Cambridge, was also working for Sir Francis Walsingham, head of the Elizabethan secret service, as a spy in France. Marlowe's other secret activity at this time was writing. Unknown to the University authorities, he translated the erotic Latin *Elegies* of Ovid, the militaristic *Pharsalia* by Lucan, and also probably wrote his play *Dido, Queen of Carthage* while at Cambridge.

1587

Marlowe, after some difficulty, becomes Master of Arts. Marlowe's frequent absences from Cambridge, occasioned by his work for Walsingham, seem to have brought him to the attention of the University authorities, for although he had fulfilled the requirements for the degree of Master of Arts, he was refused permission to proceed to that degree. It turns out that he was suspected of being a Catholic spy, and of having entered the Jesuit seminary at Rheims in order to carry out anti-government subversion. It took a sharp letter from the Queen's Privy Council itself to the University of Cambridge to set the matter straight. In 1587 Marlowe took his MA and left Cambridge for London, where he seems to have become acquainted with several influential figures. His name is often linked with the so-called 'School of Night', a circle of intellectuals centred around Sir Walter Raleigh, which had a reputation for dangerous free-thinking, and even for atheism.

1589

Marlowe arrested on a murder charge. On 18 September 1589, Marlowe was fighting with one William Bradley in Hog Lane, in the suburb of St Giles without Cripplegate. His friend, Tom Watson, a gentleman and poet (and another member of the Walsingham circle), intervened on Marlowe's behalf and, in the ensuing sword fight, Watson killed Bradley. Marlowe and Watson were arrested, and Marlowe was imprisoned in Newgate, where he remained for thirteen days, until bailed out by friends. Watson, in the meantime, had been judged to have killed in self-defence, and was remanded to prison to await the Queen's mercy – which he received in the form of a pardon the following February.

1590

'Tamburlaine the Great' published. The original performance dates of Marlowe's plays are notoriously uncertain. *Tamburlaine*, which was published in 1590, was probably first performed in 1587–88, *The Jew of Malta* in 1588–89, and *Edward II* in 1591–93. *Dido, Queen of Carthage* might have seen its first performance at any time between 1587 and 1593, and *Doctor Faustus* has been ascribed, variously, to 1588, 1589 and 1592 – the last of these dates being the one most generally accepted. Only *The Massacre at Paris* can be confidently dated – it received its first performance at the Rose theatre (where most of Marlowe's plays were staged) in January 1593. Of his dramatic works, only *Tamburlaine* was published before Marlowe's death.

1593

Death of Marlowe. In May 1593 the theatres were closed because of plague. Marlowe was staying with his patron, Thomas Walsingham (cousin of Francis), at Thomas's country house at Scadbury in Kent, when a warrant arrived for Marlowe's arrest. He appeared before the Star Chamber, the powerful judicial arm of the Privy Council, on 20 May, and was granted bail. Marlowe's arrest was occasioned by officers of the Star Chamber having searched the lodgings of his fellow playwright and former room-mate Thomas Kyd. Kyd was already in trouble politically as a co-author of the banned *Booke of Sir Thomas More*, and was now under suspicion of inciting riot. Among the papers in Kyd's room was found a manuscript copy of a heretical treatise 'Denyinge the Deity of Jhesus Christ our Savior'. Kyd insisted that the offending

11

document belonged not to him, but to Marlowe, and stuck to his story under torture. Upon Marlowe's release on bail, a government informer, Richard Baines, was given the job of preparing the case against him.

On 29 May, Baines presented to the Privy Council 'A note Containing the opinion of on[e] Christopher Marly Concerning his Damnable Judgment of Religion and scorn of god's word'. It is a list of blasphemies and treasonable opinions said to have been uttered in conversation by Marlowe. According to Baines, 'almost into every Company he Cometh he perswades men to *Atheism*', and Baines adds that 'as I think all men in Cristianity ought to indevor that the mouth of so dangerous a member may be stopped, he saith likewise that he hath quoted a number of Contrarieties out of the Scripture wch he hath giuen to some great men who in Convenient time shalbe named.'

Marlowe, then, was accused not only of holding and uttering treasonable and atheistic opinions, but of persuading others – including some 'great men who in Convenient time shalbe named' – to the same beliefs. He was, in effect, a key witness as well as a suspect in a government investigation into sedition which threatened to implicate some very powerful men. It might thus be more than just coincidence that the very next day, on 30 May, the mouth of Christopher Marlowe was indeed stopped. Still out on bail, drinking in an alehouse in Deptford, Marlowe was stabbed to death by one of his drinking companions, Ingram Frizer, a servant of Thomas Walsingham. The only witnesses were two of Marlowe's former colleagues in Francis Walsingham's secret service. The official story was that Marlowe and Frizer quarrelled over the bill, and that Marlowe attacked Frizer, who managed to disarm him and killed him in self-defence. More recently, scholars have suggested that it was a political murder, designed to protect one or more of the 'great men' with whom Marlowe had been associated.

The Theatre of Christopher Marlowe

The London theatre for which Marlowe wrote his plays was a very ambiguous establishment. At first sight, it seems like a respectable enough affair: companies of actors were named after great noblemen, proclaiming their association with the most powerful and prestigious figures in the land – Lord Leicester's Players, The Lord Chamberlain's Servants, The Lord Admiral's Men. But this very proclamation of respectability indicates an underlying insecurity about the position of the professional actor. The 'Act for the Punishment of Vagabonds' of 1572 provided that an actor could not ply his trade *unless* he belonged to a company which was under the protection of a nobleman. Any individual (or company) without such protection automatically fell into the category of vagabond, unless authorized by two judicial dignitaries. Vagabonds were potential criminals, and therefore subject to such punishments as whipping, branding or imprisonment. During the early part of the century, the relationship between a patron and his company was a real and close one, developing initially out of that between a nobleman and the minstrels of his household, who would wear his livery and be supported by his estate. As the century progressed, however, the ties between nobleman and actors tended to get looser, as acting companies became financially more and more self-sufficient. By the end of the century the patronage of a nobleman was often a legal fiction, necessitated by an out-dated law.

The financial self-sufficiency of the English theatre began in earnest in 1576. In that year, James Burbage erected what was the first permanent theatre building in England since the time of the Roman occupation. Called simply The Theatre, it stood in Shoreditch, just outside the legal boundaries of the City of London. In the next thirty years, many other playhouses were built, and theatre became a profitable commercial venture.

But while the theatre became established, it did not quite become respectable; playhouses were built outside the city boundaries because the City Fathers refused permission for them to operate within the city itself. Indeed, between 1576 and 1642 (when the theatres closed altogether for nearly twenty years during the time of the Civil War and the Protectorate) there was constant friction between the authorities of the City of London, who for the most part represented a middle-class and commercially minded sector of society who were making up the new economic order of London, and the theatre, which, in name and sometimes in fact, had the support of the aristocracy and, by the time of James I's reign, of the court as well. Various attacks were mounted by the City Fathers and by Puritan preachers against the players: they were said to distract the citizens from worship on the sabbath and from work during the week; they offended against Scripture by dressing men, or boys, in the clothes of women – for there were no actresses in England before the 1660s and all women's parts were played by boys; they were said to encourage lewdness and immorality by portraying people who acted lewdly and immorally; they attracted the baser elements of society such as thieves and prostitutes; the large gatherings often became the scene of disturbances, and at the time of plague they greatly increased the chance of an epidemic. Despite the patronage of the nobility, the London theatre in the sixteenth and early seventeenth centuries never managed to throw off its disreputable image.

The London playhouse at which most of Marlowe's plays, including *Doctor Faustus*, were staged was called the Rose, and it is a theatre about which we are comparatively well-informed, since many of the business-papers of its owner, Philip Henslowe, have been preserved. Henslowe was a businessman with many interests – indeed it is somewhat of a paradox that the City Fathers spoke so strongly against men like Henslowe, whose entrepreneurial spirit seems to have been precisely that which, in other spheres, was making London into a great mercantile centre. However, since some of Henslowe's business interests took a decidedly shady form (it is likely that he made as much money from brothels as he did from his theatrical investments) it is clear that the authorities were not entirely fanciful in some of their attacks on the disreputableness of the stage.

This, in short, was the position of the theatre in the late sixteenth century: poised uneasily between a feudal relationship with the aristocracy and an economic self-sufficiency typical of the new mercantile and entrepreneurial capitalism, its status was extraordinarily ambiguous. The successful actor might be an honoured entertainer at the courts of noblemen and even of the Queen, whereas at the other end of the scale he might be threatened with imprisonment as a vagabond, or with loss of livelihood through the prosecution of the municipal authorities. The instability and insecurity of the theatre's social position during this period may account for some of the energy and ambiguity of the drama which it produced. Politically, the theatre professional was both a privileged servant of the nobility, and also a social outsider. Within the theatre there was good reason both for a conservative bias – since the goodwill of a patron was still a necessity – and also, conversely, for a radical one, since both actor and playwright were necessarily aware that they lived on the very margins of social acceptability. Moreover, since the bread-and-butter income of an acting company came from its paying audience, it was a theatre which also needed to be sensitive to the interests and understandings of the citizens of London and the suburbs who made up that audience. It is from such tensions and contradictions that the drama of Marlowe's age emerges.

And what of the theatre buildings in which the plays of Marlowe and his contemporaries were staged? Attempts to make notional reconstructions of the playhouses of Elizabethan London have been a major pastime for theatre historians throughout this century, and disagreements abound. There was probably no 'typical' Elizabethan playhouse, and it is hard to speak in the abstract about what one might have been like. However, it is important to think about the original playing conditions in Elizabethan theatres, since these inevitably influenced the ways in which plays were written in the first place, as well as suggesting to us ways in which they might have been played. For theatres are pictures of their audiences' ideas about reality. The difference between kinds of stagings, kinds of theatres, is in part a map of how different cultures have seen the world. For example, the theatre of the late nineteenth century in Europe, the theatre which produced playwrights like Ibsen, Chekhov and Shaw, is one in which the stage suggests the necessary kind of reality required by naturalistic drama. And where does that reality essentially lie? In the detailed analysis of everyday life, in scenes which take place within families, in the drawing-rooms of the European middle classes. So the stage which we see in these plays is one which recreates in faithful detail a middle-class drawing-room so that we, the audience, can peer in through an absent fourth wall and watch the drama of everyday life being played out. What we see is an image of the truth – the natural interplay of people acting out the realities which are most important to them. Other kinds of theatre – Brechtian, Expressionist, Absurdist and so on – create other kinds of realities: the reality of an epic panorama, of the individual vision of the artist, or the reality of ritual enactment. Theatres, in the way they are set out and in the physical relationships they create between actors and audience, make symbolic statements before ever a word is spoken from the stage; they both create and reflect images of certain kinds of reality, and the plays which those theatres produce are produced in the context of such images.

What pictures of reality are painted by the theatre for which Marlowe wrote? One such picture might have been that of the theological framework of the universe itself. The canopies above the stage (the equivalent of the area which we now call 'the flies') were then referred to as 'the heavens'. Below the stage were places from which devils could emerge through trapdoors as if from hell. Many contemporary commentators made use of the analogy between the theatre and the traditional representation of the cosmos, in which heaven was above, hell below, and humanity played out its part somewhere in-between. We can only guess how strong a sense an Elizabethan audience would have had under normal conditions of this emblematic tradition, and of the stage as a cosmic diagram. The audience which first watched *Doctor Faustus*, however, must have been made aware of it quite forcibly.

Since performances took place in the afternoons, without any benefit of special stage lighting, the audience would not, as is the case now, have sat in the dark and looked upon a lighted set. In fact, many of them would probably not have sat at all, seats being more expensive, but would have stood. Seats were situated, for those who were prepared to pay extra, at the rear and sides of the theatre, and sometimes, for another additional charge, upon the stage itself, or in a 'Lord's Chamber', above and to one side of the stage. The point is a simple but important one: an Elizabethan audience was aware of itself. It could see itself more than a contemporary audience ever can or ever wishes to. Indeed, many of the satires written against the stage at this time make much of the fact that often people went to the theatre to be seen rather than to see. But the other side of the coin is that the audience's situation is not that of a passive watcher of a performance so much as that of being part of the event itself.

Theatre architecture did nothing to minimize this effect. A raised stage projected out into the middle of the yard, where the cheapest standing-space was. Spectators thus surrounded the stage on three sides, and the action was carried into the middle of the audience. Set design and stage furniture were minimal, making little effort to represent physical locations. In short, it was a theatre which, rather than inviting an audience to sit back and pretend that they were watching a 'slice of life', acknowledged its own artificiality and asked the audience to share in the creation of a fictional story.

The usual way of explaining the difference between a 'modern' theatrical experience and an Elizabethan one is this: an audience today goes to the theatre and, sitting in the dark, it pretends that it isn't an audience at all and does its best to forget itself. Latecomers, gigglers and people in tall hats are frowned upon not just because they momentarily disturb the view or hearing of another member of the audience, but because they remind the audience at the wrong time that it exists at all. There are moments in the ritual, to be sure, when the audience may recognize its own presence – notably at laugh lines and at the end of the play when it is the audience's turn to contribute by applauding – but for the most part it is self-effacing. Moreover, there is an essential dividing line between the unlit audience and the well-lit stage. At its most extreme, this division is emphasized by a proscenium arch, behind which the action takes place. During the performance, this arch serves to differentiate the 'real' world of the stage from the 'unreal' world of the audience. Anything which takes place beyond the proscenium arch (i.e., the play itself) is dramatically significant; anything which takes place in front of it (e.g., someone arriving late or leaving early) is to be ignored. For an Elizabethan audience, on the other hand, none of this would be true. They would not expect their actors to pretend that no audience was present; they would not expect anyone to attempt to persuade them that they were 'really' looking into Faustus's study; the division between the world of the play and the world of the audience would be less marked, for, although the players might be raised above the yard, none the less, the same light would shine on them all.

This description of the difference between Elizabethan and 'modern' theatre is fine up to a point, but no further. In the end, it does not really do justice to either side. Even in the most extreme cases of naturalistic theatre, an audience never actually forgets itself in the way outlined above. More importantly, the 'modern' theatre which has just been described is really rather old-fashioned: the absolute division between spectacle and spectator is less and less in evidence nowadays as theatre-in-the-round, in traverse and in promenade become more and more common. The illusionistic set is declining in popularity and theatre architects no longer design proscenium arches. For many reasons – artistic, financial, practical and ideological – audiences are becoming more familiar with a theatre which relies less on the creation of a thoroughgoing illusion, and more on an imaginative partnership between stage and audience. In many kinds of theatre, not all of them new or experimental, a direct awareness of the audience is an essential part of the experience: think of pantomimes, of one-man and one-woman shows; of agit-prop and street theatre. (In the latter case, of course, the same light shines on performer and audience alike.)

My argument is that although the differences between Elizabethan and modern theatre-goers' expectations are real and should be borne in mind, these differences are not so enormous that we need to think of the Elizabethan theatre as being some strange and exotic creature with which we have no connection. As a general point, each age has its own codes and conventions, and its own way of doing things which seem 'natural' to it. And as a specific point, many of those conventions are actually much less alien to a modern audience than we are sometimes led to believe.

I have suggested above that much of our familiarity with conventions similar to those of the Elizabethan stage comes from the area of popular theatre – the pantomime, the comic monologue and so on – rather than from that of 'high culture'. Significantly, the professional theatre of Marlowe's day also maintained a strong link with popular culture. The immense fertility of these early years of the English theatre was due in part to a merging of traditions. Cultured, well-read, University-educated men like Marlowe himself, who had been exposed to classical plays such as Seneca's tragedies, were turning to playwriting for pleasure or profit, but when they came to London they found themselves writing not just for fellow-students from the colleges of Oxford and Cambridge, but for London citizens whose own education included the popular theatre of the earlier Elizabethan period, before the opening of The Theatre in 1576. This early popular theatre, which was to be found in fairgrounds, inn yards, the great halls of noblemen's houses, and amphitheatres usually used for bull- or bear-baiting, took a variety of forms. Dramatized folk-tales, romances, biblical stories, tales from classical mythology, political and ethical satires, all contributed to the life of the theatre before 1576 – and indeed for some time after that date. But one type of play is particularly important: the morality play.

The morality play is an essentially ritualistic form of drama, having its roots in mummers' plays, which are themselves outgrowths of early fertility rituals. A typical morality play's plot is as follows: a representative Everyman-figure starts out in innocence, meets with various figures who lead him into temptation, from which he is finally redeemed by divine grace. The essential pattern is the movement from innocence to experience, and fall followed by redemption. The central function is to celebrate the truth of the Christian message, and to show it at work in the life of an archetypal human being. The story which any one particular morality play shows is repeated time after time in the lives of the audience: they are watching the plot of their own human predicament, and celebrating the happy outcome which the Christian message promises.

Despite its solemn-sounding name, and despite the essential serious-

18

ness of its subject-matter, the morality play (or 'interlude', as it was later called) is rarely dull. From its earliest appearances, the writers of morality plays seem to have kept in mind that the surest way of instructing an audience is to entertain it, and so generally the morality play has a broad, and often bawdy, comic streak. In fact, as the form developed in the sixteenth century, from street-theatre offerings into sophisticated professional entertainments, many plays which were written in the tradition of the morality actually entitled themselves 'comedies'. Moreover, the flexibility of the form was such that, as a basic dramatic pattern, it came to underlie many of the folk-tales, myths, Bible-stories and satires which were part of the early popular theatre.

In *Doctor Faustus*, Marlowe uses the morality play structure intensively. The Good and Bad Angels, the parade of the Seven Deadly Sins, the 'tempters' Valdes and Cornelius, the figure of the Old Man in the last act, who offers Faustus the chance of repentance, the comic scenes in the middle of the play – all these owe a debt to the morality tradition. The appearance on stage of the heavenly throne and of the devils reinforces this, and the story of Faustus itself is that of an inverted morality play: a man starts out in comparative innocence, falls into wicked ways, rejecting God – but is not, in the end, redeemed.

But *Doctor Faustus*, while it owes a great deal to the morality tradition, also owes much to the newer tragic drama. Tragedy in the Elizabethan and Jacobean period takes many forms: there is the tragedy of revenge, which shows someone like Hamlet placing himself outside the normal social and ethical scheme of things in order to exact justice through personal revenge. There is the tragedy of passion, in which a man is finally doomed by the destructiveness of his own emotions, passions, desires or reactions. *Othello* and *Macbeth* use this kind of pattern, and it might be argued that it is important in *Doctor Faustus* as well. Most important for our purposes, though, is the heroic tragedy, a genre which Marlowe himself might be said to have initiated in his earlier *Tamburlaine* plays. Tamburlaine, starting out as a simple shepherd, becomes a mighty emperor. We see his rise and fall, and the central concern of the tragedy is the paradoxical nature of human existence which decrees that a man so full of energy and potential must nonetheless die. The key phrase is spoken by Tamburlaine himself when he finally comes to realize that, 'Tamburlaine, the scourge of God, must die'.

A morality play shows the human condition in the context of a unified cosmos, in which heaven and hell hold their rightful places and the world of mankind is structured in relation to them, in which the stars circulate in fixed orbit around an earth which is the centre of the universe;

the emphasis is on the optimism of the Christian message of redemption. A heroic tragedy such as *Tamburlaine*, on the other hand, concentrates on mankind not as part of a great cosmic process but as something which sets itself up in opposition to that process. To put it at its baldest, if a morality play shows the life and death of a protagonist in generalized, allegorical terms, inviting an audience to experience the ways in which God's grace triumphs over the sins of the flesh, and viewing death as something to be celebrated, a tragedy shows the life and death of a protagonist in specific terms, inviting an audience to experience the essential loneliness of the central character, and viewing death as something to be mourned.

Thus the morality play and the tragedy are more than just two different dramatic forms: they represent two different ways of looking at the world. The first, medieval in origin, integrative and comic in spirit, states broadly that, 'mankind is frail and subject to temptation, but redeemable by God's grace'. The second, more sceptical, questioning and secular, and more concerned with the ultimate disintegration and destruction of individual human aspirations, says, 'what happens when people set themselves outside the established order of things? See how vulnerable they are – but see also how the universe looks from their point of view.' In *Doctor Faustus*, by combining elements of morality play and tragedy, Marlowe sets these two visions of the human predicament against each other.

One of my main propositions about *Doctor Faustus* will be that it offers us a double perspective on Faustus himself: on the one hand he is presented as a version of a morality-play protagonist – his story is told in a cosmic context, against a background of the traditional, orthodox universe in which, by persisting in his occultism, he is doomed to damnation unless he can find a way to repent. On the other hand, we also see him as a tragic figure, heroically challenging that very universe, calling its truths into doubt, and asserting his own individual identity in opposition to traditional orthodoxy. This is not a revolutionary reading of the play: many critics have discussed *Doctor Faustus* in terms of its relationship to these two traditions, of morality and tragedy. Often, critics have found it useful to opt for one or the other of these perspectives as being the 'correct' one, and thus to argue that *Doctor Faustus* is essentially a morality play, or essentially a heroic tragedy. My own belief is that it is 'essentially' a play which exploits the tension between these two ways of perceiving the world.

When critics disagree, as they do about *Doctor Faustus*, their usual recourse is to 'turn to the text' in order to prove that their reading of it is correct. In the case of *Doctor Faustus*, however, this is less easy than it sounds, since many of the areas of disagreement about *Doctor Faustus* relate to the questions of what the real text of the play actually is, and who wrote which parts of it. To understand this, we need to consider the way in which the text has been handed down to us.

It is self-evident that the text of a play is different in kind from that of a novel. A novelist writes in order to be published, and his or her medium of communication with the audience is the printed word. With one or two notable exceptions this is not the case with a playwright, who writes lines that will be spoken by actors, and whose initial medium of communication is the performance. For the playwright, publication is almost always a secondary issue, however desirable it may be thought to be.

In Marlowe's day this was even more true than it is today: printing the texts of plays which had appeared on the London stage was a new form of publishing venture, and the remarkable thing about it is not that we have lost so many plays from the Elizabethan period, but that we have retained so many. Certainly, then as now, many more plays were performed than were ever published. Marlowe himself lived to see only one of his plays, *Tamburlaine*, printed. The earliest edition of *Doctor Faustus* is dated 1604, eleven years after Marlowe's death. In 1616 another version of the play was printed which differs considerably from the 1604 edition. To make matters even more complicated, we know from the evidence of Henslowe's papers that in 1602 he had paid two lesser-known writers, William Bird and Samuel Rowley, four pounds, 'for ther adicyones in doctor fostes'. Four pounds, incidentally, was a considerable sum of money in 1602: it represented more than Henslowe was generally willing to pay for a new play at this time. The additions made by Bird and Rowley must have been quite sizeable.

Thus, before the play was ever printed, script doctors had been called in to add certain scenes, and while we do not know for sure that these additions were incorporated into the printed text either in 1604 or 1616, it seems quite possible that they were. A further complexity arises in that many scholars have suspected that other writers besides Bird and Rowley might have contributed to the play, either with or without Marlowe's knowledge and approval. The problem is therefore a double one: we have two texts, two versions in effect, of the play, and we do not know exactly which parts of either version were actually written by Marlowe himself – although it should be added that there is a general consensus that most of the non-farcical material in Acts I and II and Act V belongs to him.

Let us deal first, then, with this question of authorship, and think about what it means to the way we read the play. We must accept that the play which we think of as Marlowe's *Doctor Faustus* is actually not just by Marlowe, but by Marlowe and some other writers who collaborated with him during his lifetime, or who amended and added to the text after he had sold it to the acting company, perhaps even after his death. This does not seem to me to present a great problem. It is true that if certain evidence comes to light in the future about who wrote which parts, and if we have made certain arguments about Marlowe's thought, beliefs or dramatic technique based on some passage which later turns out to have been written by Samuel Rowley, we might feel slightly foolish – but that is all. Collaboration was a common mode of dramatic authorship in the Elizabethan and Jacobean theatre (there are signs that it is becoming so again today), and it is perfectly possible that many of the non-Marlovian scenes and passages were included with Marlowe's approval. Even if this is not the case – if, for example, they were added by Bird and Rowley after his death – this seems to me to be true to the general fate of a dramatic text. A playscript, once it leaves the hands of the playwright and comes into the possession of an acting company, becomes the property of that company as much as that of the playwright. Under Elizabethan law, which did not include the notion of copyright, this was even more the case than it is today; but today, too, lines are changed, whole scenes rewritten in rehearsal, and even from performance to performance ('That line didn't work, we'll have to cut it'; 'This act is far too long, we need to shorten this speech'; 'We need something here to show how he gets from A to B'). Ideally, of course, the original writer will perform that task, but if that writer is not available (because dead?) it is not unusual for someone else to act as script doctor. We are used to speculating about the original intentions of an author in writing such-and-such a line or such-and-such a speech; when dealing with Elizabethan plays, however, it is perhaps more realistic, if we need to think about intentions at all, to consider those of the company which first presented the play.

In short, I see no reason to be put off by the multiplicity of authors of *Doctor Faustus*. The only disadvantage it confers on the play is that critics who like some parts of *Doctor Faustus* but not others, or who find that the play lacks unity, are provided with a ready-made explanation which I find over-simplistic: 'Marlowe wrote this scene, which I like, but not that scene, which I don't,' is a common way of arguing. The assumption, of course, is that the other writers were noticeably inferior to Marlowe. As I intend to show in my analysis of the middle parts of the play (which are the ones most often attributed to a collaborator), whoever contributed to *Doctor Faustus* understood the play very well, and knew precisely what they were doing.

The second question – that of there being two separate texts of the play – is more vexing, and here we are taken back to the tension which exists in *Doctor Faustus* between tragedy and morality play. To put it at its most simple, the 1604 edition (commonly called the A-text) looks most like a tragedy; the 1616 edition (the B-text) looks most like a morality. Any modern edition which we read today is an amalgam of the A- and B-texts.

In fact, most modern editors tend to base their editions on the B-text, for a series of reasons. Firstly, it is longer: it contains several comic scenes which the A-text does not, and also a greater number of scenes in which the powers of hell are portrayed on stage. This helps to give the B-text its stronger flavour of the morality play. The B-text therefore has the advantage of inclusivity. Also, it is now thought to be the more original of the two versions, despite being printed at a later date. The most common explanation of the difference between the two is that the A-text represents a shortened version of the play which had been designed specifically for the acting company to take on tour in the provinces, where they would be performing in places where the facilities for grand theatrical effects, such as the supernatural machinery, would not be available. The theatrically more ambitious B-text is thought to be the one performed in London at the Rose, which could cope with large props like descending thrones and opening hell-mouths more satisfactorily. While this is a conjecture, it has a ring of plausibility to it.

There is, however, no way of saying that one or the other of these versions represents the 'real' *Doctor Faustus*. Indeed, the very concept of a 'real' *Doctor Faustus* is open to question, since, as I have suggested, changes made to meet different playing conditions are an integral part of the life of a playscript. I am left with the sense that Marlowe's company, in playing *Doctor Faustus*, thought of the script not as an immutable article of holy writ, but as a fluid, changeable entity which could be adapted to suit their various playing needs. In having the two texts, A and B, handed down to us, we are in a position to see two different stages of that fluid process. Neither is more 'real' than the other, nor are these two the only possible versions of *Doctor Faustus* – different audiences, different playing spaces, would probably have demanded further adaptations which never found their way into print. The various uncertainties concerning the text of *Doctor Faustus*, I would argue, serve to remind us of the peculiar nature of *any* printed dramatic text, but most especially of one from the Elizabethan and Jacobean period: the published text represents not a definitive edition of a playscript, but an opportunistic spin-off from a successful performance or series of performances.

Yet for our present purposes, we need a common point of reference. Recently there has been a call among some Marlowe scholars for *Doctor Faustus* to be studied not as a single play made up of an amalgamation of the two texts, but as two separate plays, *Doctor Faustus A* and *Doctor Faustus B*. I have a certain amount of sympathy for this approach, since it avoids falsely privileging one version over the other, and it also acknowledges that the stories told by the two versions differ from each other in several respects.

However, there are good reasons for not rejecting the modern editions which have amalgamated the A- and B-texts. The call to study *Doctor Faustus* as two separate plays is partly a purist one; it implies that modern editors are obscuring our view of the true, original *Doctor Faustus*. But, as I have already suggested, this true original is itself a phantom. We have in our possession a play from the late Elizabethan age called *Doctor Faustus*. It was created through collaboration, probably changed many times during its early stage history, it found its way into print on two separate occasions and in two separate forms in the early seventeenth century, and since then various editors have attempted, with varying degrees of success, to make dramatic sense out of the original documents. They have, by and large, come to a degree of consensus, so that the differences between one modern edition and another are relatively slight. These editors are as much a part of the authentic history of the play as are the original publishers of the first and second editions. The play which we read, which we see acted, has been created not just by Christopher Marlowe, nor even by Christopher Marlowe and his anonymous Elizabethan collaborators and script doctors. It has also been created by modern editors, through the choices which they have made out of a mass of conflicting material.

In this study, therefore, I have followed convention in using a modern critical edition. (Quotations and act, scene and line references relate to Roma Gill's edition of *Doctor Faustus*, published by Norton Books in their New Mermaids series; in Appendix Two I have provided a table of cross-references to other easily available editions. I have also, for the sake of brevity, followed convention in referring to the author as 'Marlowe' throughout.) In this study I will, occasionally, be taking into account some of the conflicting meanings which are to be derived from the alternative versions of the play which have existed in the past.

However, my main interest lies in examining the kinds of meaning which may be produced from the text which we commonly read, of the play of multiple authorship which we agree to call Marlowe's *Doctor Faustus*.

The Play

The prologue

Why does a writer begin a play with a prologue? What is the point, before a play begins, of having somebody, not a character in the main action of the play, but a kind of narrator, story-teller or master of ceremonies, come forward and make a series of introductory remarks about what the audience is going to see? What is the intended effect, and what does it do to the way the audience responds to the main action once that starts?

There are a series of possible answers to these questions, and not all of them will apply in every instance. One reason might be for clarity – to make sure that the spectators know, in broad outline, what it is that they are going to spend the next few hours watching. It may be an announcement, to establish that the play is beginning, or a kind of advertisement – what television writers now call a 'teaser', the dramatic equivalent of the publisher's dustcover précis, designed to whet the reader's appetite. It may be to give the audience some kind of objectivity: to remind them that what they are about to see *is* a play and to provide what the twentieth-century dramatist Bertolt Brecht called 'alienation' – the necessary detachment which allows us to analyse what we are experiencing in the theatre as well as being absorbed by it. Or it might be to tell the audience how they should react to what they are about to see. This might be done on the very basic level of establishing a genre: as a friend might establish before telling a story that what follows will be a joke, or an account of something terrible that happened to him today – so that even in the early stages of the narrative we can decode it according to the spirit in which it is told, and avoid making elementary mistakes of interpretation (say, by laughing as he tells us how he fell from the first-floor window – a permissible reaction if we perceive the story to be a joke, but not if he is trying to enlist our sympathy for the terrible day he's just had).

How, then, does Marlowe use this device of starting the play off with a prologue? He uses it, I think, for all of the reasons listed above. The first few lines, it seems, belong to the category of advertisement and appetite-whetter, and the effect is twofold. Firstly, while denying that *this* play is going to be like anything the audience is accustomed to see at this theatre, the prologue also has the effect of linking *Doctor Faustus* with plays about 'marching', 'sporting' and 'pomp'. Secondly, of course, there is the suggestion that what the audience is going to see will actually be *better* than the usual fare. The tone is mock-apologetic and the implication is that the writer could easily turn his hand to such tales if he had a mind to. Indeed he could – 'dalliance of love / in courts of kings' sounds very much like Marlowe's own *Edward II*, while 'the pomp of proud audacious deeds' is his *Tamburlaine* to a 'T'. This time, however, the implication goes, the writer has something rather special to impart. But notice that it is all done *by* implication. Stories of warriors and lovers and kings are tossed aside as if they were easily dealt with, but the direct advertisement is also low-key: 'Only this, Gentles – we must now perform / The form of Faustus' fortunes, good or bad.' If the language of the first few lines is overwritten, tending to parody the 'heavenly verse' to which the author lays claim, then these following ones, as he reaches the real subject of his sentence, are almost an anti-climax, a throw-away.

We should be aware that even at this early stage Marlowe is playing with the audience. If one function of the prologue might be to tell the audience how to react to the main action, Marlowe appears at this stage to be deliberately drawing back from any comment on the story: 'Faustus' fortunes, *good or bad*' – as if the speaker of the prologue doesn't know and the audience shouldn't be told! But this is disingenuous, for even the first-night (or first-afternoon, as it would have been) audience of *Doctor Faustus* in the 1590s would probably have known something of the story before they saw anything of the play itself. They would have known, in particular, that it was the story of the man who sold his soul to the Devil and was damned for it.

This is even more true of a twentieth-century audience, of course. The name of Faustus has resonances even for those who have never seen the play, for it has been assimilated into our mythologies. Just as we know, without having read a word of Dickens, that Scrooge was a miser, and just as we know, without having seen the Shakespeare play, that Romeo and Juliet are lovers who come to a tragic end, so we know that among our inherited archetypes is the one of the man who sold his soul to the Devil, and that his name was Faustus.

Marlowe, of course, was one of the creators of that myth – it is because of his work (and that of Goethe, Thomas Mann and others) that the myth exists for us in the way that it does. But he did not create it out of nothing. In Marlowe's day, too, the story of a man's compact with the Devil was familiar stuff. Such tales dated back at least to New Testament times: a man called Simon Magus, first mentioned in the Acts of the Apostles, is a prototype for Faustus. The story, however, took on fresh impetus in the early sixteenth century, when references began to appear to a historical Faust, an itinerant scholar whose doings served as a focus for stories of occultism. Named alternately Georg or Johannes Faustus, he became after his death the hero of a popular German 'biography', published in 1587. This in turn was translated into English by 1592, and it is this English translation which Marlowe read, and which he used as his primary source for *Doctor Faustus*. We know this to be the case because several passages added by the English translator and not to be found in the German original, are found also in Marlowe's play.

Thus for Marlowe's audience, too, the story of Faustus and the devilish contract was not altogether new. The use of the Chorus to pre-empt the action is a little deceptive: the prologue is not providing an audience with totally new information so much as reminding them of things they may already know, in part at least. The apparent ingenuousness of the phrase, 'Faustus' fortunes, good or bad', is less innocent and more ironical than it first seems. It is, in fact, an early example of an ironic tone which will recur throughout the play.

How much, then, does the prologue actually tell us? It starts off with an account of Faustus's early life. The small detail that he was 'born, of parents base of stock' is significant. It is included, one might suppose, to make Faustus's rise to power more dramatic, but its secondary effect is to introduce the political and social dimension of the Elizabethan sin of pride: Faustus is, among other things, an upstart, a man who refuses to accept his place. As in *Tamburlaine*, the story of a humble man's rise to great power is being told, but now it is being told in metaphysical rather than imperialistic terms. The prologue goes on to recount Faustus's rise to academic eminence, his ability to debate theology and philosophy – and here the language begins to get more obviously manipulative of the audience's response. Now, it seems, Faustus is 'swollen with cunning of a self-conceit' (little doubt here as to how we should respond!); the image of the waxen wings conjures up the story of Icarus, whose story was commonly used in the Renaissance to illustrate the folly and danger of excessive pride and ambition. We are told, moreover, that, 'heavens conspired [Faustus's] overthrow'. In fact, the Chorus seems to have told us the whole story of *Doctor Faustus* in about seven lines: he was conceited, over-ambitious in trying to bargain with the devil, and heaven punished him for it by allowing the devil to take his soul. The next words seem to confirm that reading – 'For falling ...': the image of the waxen wings which have now melted from the heat of the sun leaves us with the obvious next stage. The man who hoped they would carry him is falling – an image, of course, of Faustus's damnation – he is 'falling' into hell.

But things are not quite as simple as this. For 'falling' here does not mean 'dropping to earth because of gravity'. Look at the whole clause: 'For falling to a devilish exercise, / And glutted now with learning's golden gifts, / He surfeits upon cursed necromancy.' The Chorus is not talking about the *end* of Faustus's career as a devil-worshipper at all; in fact he is talking about the very beginning of it. To 'fall to' something, in Elizabethan colloquial speech, means to begin it. It is most often used with meals – one 'falls to dinner'. The Chorus is not talking about some time in the future when Faustus 'falls' from his position of worldly power, or gets dragged down into hell; he is talking about 'now' – the moment when the play starts. The last line of the prologue makes this clear: 'And this the man that in his study sits'; the Chorus gestures towards the figure on stage sitting in his study, and the action proper begins.

There are three reasons why this apparently trivial example of word-play is worth spending time on. First of all, because it shows how carefully one must attend to some of Marlowe's language. Very often he is not saying quite what he seems to be saying: in *Doctor Faustus* words often change their meanings, just as 'falls' here changes its meaning from the seemingly obvious sense of 'drops to earth', to the less obvious meaning of 'begins', which then generates other words connected with feeding: 'glutted' and 'surfeits'. And *Doctor Faustus* is, among other things, a play about a man who is supposed to be good with words ('Excelling all; whose sweet delight disputes / In th' heavenly matters of theology'), but who mistakes – fatally – the meaning of much of what is told him by the agents of hell.

Secondly, the particular shift of meaning that 'falls' undergoes is a typical one in the play, one which is often used to a particular end, and one for which we should be on the look-out. It is the shift of meaning between the levels of literalism and metaphor. What seems to be the literal meaning of 'falling to earth' suddenly turns out to be the metaphorical level of 'falling to dinner'. This is complicated by the fact that it is itself set within the metaphorical picture of Faustus-as-Icarus. A movement between the literal level of meaning and the metaphorical level, and the momentary confusion which this creates, is a repeated feature of the play. Moreover, it is a thematically significant feature. The play itself deals with the very boundaries of man's knowledge. Heaven

29

and hell – are the pictures that are conventionally painted of them real? Is hell *really* beneath the ground, staffed by devils with pitchforks and pointed tails? Or is this just a fictional picture of it, one which has been made up to make hell seem more comprehensible or more vivid – a metaphor, in fact? Time after time we will see meanings shift backwards and forwards across the barrier between the metaphorical and the literal, until the nature of reality itself is called into question. And, of course, the nature of reality is one of the things which Faustus himself is attempting to comprehend.

Thirdly (and this is quite closely connected with the previous point), the effect that this has on the audience is of a kind of double-take as regards the time-scale of what the Chorus is talking about. He seems at first to be talking about the whole of Faustus's career; then we realize that he is talking about a specific moment when Faustus begins his researches into black magic, and that he is going to leave it to the main dramatic action to tell the rest of the story. To create this momentary uncertainty about the time-scale so early in the play, and through the mouth of the seemingly objective Chorus, is a kind of foreshadowing of later developments in the play, where Marlowe uses the magic of the stage and the magic of his own language to distort the usual realities of both time and space. By the time we reach the last soliloquy, in fact, time will have been distorted to the lineaments of Faustus's own psyche.

'And this the man that in his study sits': by the end of the prologue Marlowe has advertised his wares; he has given us a taste of what awaits (we know it is to be a story of black magic and we know something about the main character's 'self-conceit'); he has hinted as to how we should react to him; and he has also presented him as an object for our contemplation rather than as a hero with whom we are immediately to identify. But while the conventions of the Elizabethan theatre in general, and of this play in particular, work to discourage identification with the hero, Marlowe will also, as the play develops, allow us insights into the workings of the hero's mind in a way which no other writer had ever attempted in the English theatre.

Faustus's first soliloquy
(Act I, Scene 1, ll. 1–62)

As the scene shifts from the external, critical and manipulative presence of the Chorus, to be replaced by the famous first soliloquy of Faustus himself, we perform a movement which is to become characteristic of the play – the movement from objectivity (the convention of the seemingly detached voice of the Chorus in his monologue, telling us *about* Faustus) to subjectivity (the convention of soliloquy, in which a character expresses his inmost thoughts). The movement between objective and subjective realities is an important feature of the play because one of the major questions which the play addresses is the idea of a double perspective on Faustus. We are asked to see him in two conflicting ways throughout the play. On the one hand we see him from, as it were, the outside, sitting detachedly in judgement on his follies as the prologue suggests we should. On the other hand, however, we are often drawn into a much closer and more sympathetic relationship with him, and are asked to understand him from the inside. It is the tension, and even the opposition, between these two views of Faustus which has sparked some of the main critical controversies about the play, and which gives the play so much of its energy.

Just because Faustus is speaking a soliloquy, however, does not mean that we need accept everything he has to say uncritically. In fact, his first speech here is a masterpiece of off-key rhetoric. He stands at the crux of his career, and systematically rejects the conventional branches of Renaissance learning. The first to go is 'Analytics' – Aristotelian philosophy. At first we are told that this has 'ravished' Faustus, but within a few lines it has been dismissed as unworthy of his attention. The transition is effected by singling out one line of Aristotle: '*Bene disserere est finis logices*' ('To dispute well is the aim of logic'). And at this point Faustus is brought up short, asking:

> Affords this art no greater miracle?
> Then read no more, thou hast attained that end;
> A greater subject fitteth Faustus' wit.

Two details about this short extract are significant. First of all, Faustus's specific (and automatic?) choice of vocabulary: he is looking already, even if ironically, for 'miracles'. Secondly, Faustus is claiming, in one of the first things he says, almost as a matter of course, to have mastered the art of logic: it will be instructive to keep that belief of Faustus's in mind as we follow his fortunes through the play.

It is worth noticing, too, that Faustus's dismissal of 'Analytics' is based on a minor error in translation.

> *Bene disserere est finis logices.*
> Is to dispute well logic's chiefest end?

In translating *disserere* simply as 'to dispute', Faustus is being inexact: 'dispute' as a translation of *disserere* must be taken in its widest sense, to mean not just skill in debate, but the ability to reason accurately about truth. Faustus's contemptuous use of the word 'dispute' shows that he takes the word in its most limited meaning – and in doing so shows himself to be a bad logician. The mistake is small, but it is significant: from the very beginning, words and their meanings present a problem for Faustus.

Next to be rejected is medicine – and we see that Faustus's bad characteristics do not appear to be limited to self-conceit. There is a touch of avarice here too, for as he considers the career of physician, his thoughts naturally turn to the notion that a medical career will allow him to 'heap up gold'. However, his next thought, of being 'eternized for some wondrous cure' again suggests the superhuman longings for a kind of immortality which will lead Faustus into league with the Devil. Once more, though, a single phrase is enough to quench his enthusiasm; once more the reason given is that Faustus has already achieved the end prescribed – he is already a famous physician, and he demands more. And once more, he is looking for miracles – now the miracle of making 'men to live eternally, / Or, being dead, raise them to life again'. Faustus's subconscious aspirations are being suggested to the audience long before he himself announces them.

The law does not really get a look-in. At least logic and medicine were rejected in terms of their own self-justifications. But opening Justinian's *Institutes*, Faustus sees nothing but 'A petty case of paltry legacies'. The 'servile and illiberal' discipline of law is consigned to the dustbin, without argument.

It is at this point that the self-proclaimed master of logic makes a great logical error. In his rejection of medicine and the law, Faustus might have been expressing a dissatisfaction with what the subjects had to offer. We might feel a certain sympathy, too, with his more contentious dismissal of analytics. But when Faustus turns to divinity, his vaunted logic really betrays him.

> Jerome's Bible Faustus, view it well.
> *Stipendium peccati mors* est: ha! *Stipendium, etc*
> The reward of sin is death. That's hard.
> *Si peccasse negamus, fallimur, et nulla est in nobis veritas.*
> If we say that we have no sin, we deceive ourselves
> and there is no truth in us. Why then, belike, we
> must sin, and so consequently die.
> Ay, we must die, an everlasting death.
> What doctrine call you this? . . .

Faustus's syllogism of sin and death is a fine joke on Marlowe's part – and an excellent example of the way in which meaning may be distorted by detaching words from their proper contexts. There are two basic flaws in Faustus's reasoning. Firstly, the texts which he chooses are crucially and famously incomplete. The first, Romans VI:23, reads in full:

For the wages of sin is death; but the gift of God is eternal life through Jesus Christ our Lord. (Authorized Version)

The second, I John I:8–9, runs:

If we say that we have no sin, we deceive ourselves, and the truth is not in us. If we confess our sins, he is faithful and just to forgive us our sins, and to cleanse us from all unrighteousness.

In both cases, then, Faustus has chosen only the first part of the statement, omitting the vital second half, which contains the idea of God's mercy and the redeeming power of Christ. He has missed out, that is to say, the entire New Testament story! Any moderately informed member of Marlowe's original audience probably knew these biblical passages, literally, 'chapter and verse'; certainly the audience would have known the gist of them, and would have known that Faustus's interpretation of Scripture was flying in the face of orthodox Christianity.

The second flaw in Faustus's reasoning is one which is recognizable even without any specific textual knowledge of the Bible. Faustus's syllogism is only superficially valid. Certainly, it has a surface persuasiveness: point A in conjunction with point B leads to point C; the reward of sin is death, we are all sinners, therefore we must all die. But Faustus adds a crucial rider to his syllogism: 'Ay, we must die an everlasting death.' But that word, 'everlasting', is not in the original equation! It does not take a sophisticated theologian to spot the inconsistency in Faustus's logic. Certainly, according to orthodox Christian doctrine, we are all sinners. Certainly, according to common experience, we are all going to die. But not necessarily 'an *everlasting* death'. In fact, the very purpose of the passages from the New Testament which Faustus so resolutely ignores is to affirm that death is *not* 'everlasting'. It is a significant word for Faustus to have added: compare his thoughts, when talking of medicine, of being 'eternized', and of making 'men to live eternally'. Notions of eternity pulse through Faustus's thoughts continually.

Having rejected the permissible branches of learning – logic, medicine,

law and divinity – Faustus turns to black magic with the following
words:

> Divinity adieu!
> These metaphysics of magicians,
> And necromantic books are heavenly.

And that one word, 'heavenly', sets up a whole series of reverberations.
It contains in itself two perspectives: firstly, what Faustus might mean
by it, and secondly, what we might read into it. Faustus clearly means
something good by it; 'heavenly', for him, has the sense of 'beautiful', or
'attractive'. These necromantic books, he means us to understand, are
all that he desires. But what a superbly wrong choice of word to express
the thought! For 'heavenly' is precisely what they are not: 'hellish' is
what they are. The word 'heavenly' is so glaringly wrong that we must be
expected to notice it – and in noticing it (as we have just noticed the
falsity of Faustus's syllogism about the reward of sin) we are to be
alerted to the relationship between us as audience, and Faustus on the
stage – which is that, typically, we know more than he does. Faustus
misses the ambiguity of his own language, is unaware of the sub-text
which is already crying out that he is mistaken in his assumptions. We
do not.

'Heavenly' and 'heavens' are words which Faustus often gets wrong,
or makes mistakes about, or understands only half-completely. 'Heavens'
had the same double meaning in Elizabethan times as it does today –
referring either to the Christian heaven, or simply to the skies. In later
scenes, when Faustus and Mephostophilis debate cosmology, these two
meanings are sometimes distinguished from each other and sometimes
not. Faustus learns about the literal heavens of astronomy, but not
about the heaven of theology. And here, in his first soliloquy, he uses the
word 'heavenly' in a metaphorical sense, while the literal sense of the
word proclaims his wrong-headedness.

I suggested earlier that when we turned from the prologue to this
soliloquy, we moved from an objective standpoint to a subjective one.
But in fact this is only partly true. Certainly, we have been 'seeing into'
the recesses of Faustus's soul, and learning his inmost thoughts. To that
extent, our relationship with him is more intimate than it was during the
Chorus's speech. But we have seen a man whose innermost thoughts (at
this moment) consist of a series of logical arguments which are so flawed
that we, the audience, are asked to be aware of their falsity. That is to
say, we are detached from him to some extent, still looking at him rather
critically. This detached and alienated position which an audience tends

to have towards Faustus during the early part of this first soliloquy is reinforced by the balanced, considered rhythms of his speech. Faustus is being analytical, and an audience tends to respond analytically; if he provides a kind of logic in his speech, an audience begins to search out the logical objections to what he has to say.

Once he begins to talk about the 'metaphysics of magicians', however, the rhythms change. We are swung into the rapturous cadences of Faustus's imaginings of the 'world of profit and delight' which awaits him. This crescendo of the imagination, which starts with the 'studious artisan', and moves through 'Emperors and kings' to the infinity of the 'mind of man', leads finally to the inevitable point of, first, 'mighty god' (in the A-text; the B-text has 'demi-god') and then (in both texts and unmistakably), 'deity'. But at this point, ambiguity again emerges, even in the midst of rapture. Faustus's 'mighty god', 'demi-god' or 'deity' for him at that moment represents power – the ultimate power that he can imagine. But against this must be set an awareness of the oneness of the Christian God; not 'a deity', but *the* deity, whose command is, 'Thou shalt have no other gods before me', and whose presence ultimately defines the rules of the game which Faustus is about to play. Far from gaining a deity, Faustus's brains will be put to the task of losing one.

I would suggest, then, that during the first few minutes of the play, the audience's relationship with Faustus is continually changing. We start off detached, being told *about* him by the Chorus. We are then shown the workings of his mind, but still remain comparatively detached, analysing his arguments. As he becomes more rapturous, we are invited to share more intimately his vision – but even as Marlowe offers that intimacy, he also undercuts it. The essential movement is between a sympathetic response and an ironic one.

This raises the question of the relationship between these two responses. An author may relate them in a variety of ways – for example, an audience may begin by sympathizing with a character, then, as the story develops, they may be turned against him. Or the author may begin by depicting a character ironically, and then go into greater detail to bring an audience to feel greater sympathy for the character. In both cases, there is the implication that the second of these two responses, the one which an audience comes to later, is the more developed, considered and therefore the more correct response. On the other hand, the audience may be asked *not* to make a choice between two opposing interpretations, but to explore a position in which the indeterminacy of the point of view is the whole point of the story. In *Doctor Faustus*, the way in which we view the relationship between irony and sympathy will play an important part in determining how we respond to the play as a whole.

The Good and Bad Angels
(Act I, Scene 1, ll. 69–76)

We have had two set speeches so far, but no interaction between characters – none of the stuff of which drama is essentially made. Now, as another character, Wagner, appears on stage, it seems as if the drama proper is about to start. This. however, is not quite the case. What happens next is little more than an interruption – in fact, a double interruption – of the monologue. Faustus's command to Wagner to bring Valdes and Cornelius merely sets the stage for their introduction. The more important interruption comes from the Good and Bad Angels. But what kind of interruption is it?

It is one which changes the whole mood of the play – indeed, it changes the very kind of play which we are watching. During the first two long speeches, the audience's relationship with Faustus was, on the whole, becoming more intimate. The appearance of the Good and Bad Angels on the stage is calculated to shatter that sense of involvement. For they bring with them the trappings and structure of a kind of drama which imposes a definite 'meaning' on the events of the story – the structure of the morality play. By bringing on stage these essential props of an older dramatic tradition, Marlowe also puts on stage the beliefs with which that tradition was associated. They represent the belief, while they are on stage, that the 'reality' of the universe is the traditional cosmic diagram in which man is poised between heaven and hell, and the powers of each do battle for his soul. The urgings of the Good and Bad Angels have this as their main point and justification: they add, not extra information, but an extra perspective. If, in listening to Faustus's soliloquy, we were tempted to see him as an autonomous individual, the presence of the Good and Bad Angels insists now that we see him in the perspective of eternity, and in the context of the traditional Christian cosmology, wherein he is but one part of a larger pattern.

The protagonist of a morality play typically comes up against a series of allegorical figures. Some of these figures may be seen as 'characters' in their own right – 'other people', or external influences which a person comes up against in the course of his or her life. Others, however, may be projections of the protagonist's own personality. In the play *Everyman*, for example, the hero meets and talks with 'Good-Deeds', a figure who represents part of his own character. It has been the subject of some debate as to whether the Angels in *Doctor Faustus* should be seen as external characters, or as symbolic representations of Faustus's own personality. In his 1974 production of the play for the Royal Shakespeare Company, director John Barton had the parts of the Good and Bad Angels 'played' by puppets, operated by Faustus himself and with Faustus speaking their lines. The implication was that they were simply mouthpieces for Faustus's own thoughts.

This is a perfectly viable way of thinking about the Good and Bad Angels, and one that does not conflict with the implications of the morality play tradition which they represent. After all, it is not so great a step to imagine the supernatural inhabiting (or 'possessing') the psyche, rather than appearing outside it; it certainly need not contradict the idea that the Angels represent some reality which is other than Faustus's own consciousness. It does seem to me, though, that to interpret the Angels solely as being manifestations of Faustus's thoughts does create problems later in the play, when they reappear. I am happier with a view of the Angels which locates them outside Faustus's head. It is worth noticing that in this scene he does not even appear to hear them talking – although I have seen this fact used to argue, perfectly plausibly, that they represent inner voices, voices of his subconscious or his conscience.

It may be that here, as in so many other places in the play, the ambiguity is the very point. I argued earlier that one of the key movements of the play occurred between the linguistic levels of literalism and metaphor. Perhaps this dichotomy exists in the figures of the Angels, and we are meant to be in a state of doubt as to whether they are really, literally 'there', or whether they are projections of Faustus's own personality – metaphors, in fact, for what is going on in his head.

There is one further interpretative problem about the Angels. I have suggested that, because they bring with them the suggestions of the morality play, their presence on stage is quite a serious one, reminding the audience of a larger reality. There is, however, another way of thinking about them. Because they come from an old – and even perhaps an outmoded – dramatic tradition, might an audience have greeted them, in the 1590s, with laughter? Might they, in this first appearance at least, have seemed rather comical figures to Marlowe's audience, outdated representatives of a tradition that was being perceived as rather clichéd? (As if, in a modern play, someone were to come on and say, 'Anyone for tennis?') I am not sure how far this idea can be taken, but it is an interesting speculation that Marlowe might have initially introduced some hackneyed figures from the morality plays in order to mock that tradition, rather than to claim its support. If this is the intended effect, though, it is short-lived, for as the play progresses it becomes increasingly difficult to treat the figures from the old moralities lightheartedly. By their last appearance, nobody is laughing at the Angels.

This first appearance, in any case, is a brief one, and it makes very little impression on Faustus. When he speaks again, it is in a continuation of his previous flight of fancy. The imagination creates the aspirations – and despite such warning words as 'glutted', Marlowe now encourages his audience to abandon themselves to Faustus's rhetoric. This speech generates once more the naïve sympathy which we must have for Faustus if the play is going to work in the multi-dimensional way which, at its best, it does. Once more the aspirations of Faustus work to carry us along with them, through the richness of the language and the exuberance of the rhythms. But once more, too, there is an undercurrent of irony. For what a strange set of aspirations they are! They veer between the intellectual and the sensual, and occasionally they confuse the two completely. The words 'glutted with conceit' summon up the twin resonances of the sensual and the intellectual, and the next two lines have precisely the same effect, as Faustus imagines spirits who, on the one hand, will fetch him what he pleases, and who on the other hand will resolve him of all ambiguities. 'Pleasant fruits' and 'strange philosophy' follow quickly one upon the other, the latter degenerating immediately into cheap gossip – 'the secrets of all foreign kings'. The most telling detail is Faustus's confusion of the spheres of intellect and luxury, as he vows, 'I'll have them fill the public schools with silk, / Wherewith the students shall be bravely clad.' The joke is threefold: firstly, it is a jibe against the University statutes which had ordered undergraduates of Marlowe's time to dress plainly. Secondly, and more pointedly, Faustus, in his imagination, reverses the traditional association between scholars and poverty, and clothes the scholars of Wittenberg in silk – giving them the worldly signs of status which they normally lack. But thirdly, the joke is against Faustus himself; in his shortsightedness it seems that Faustus, even as he dreams of the ultimate worldly power, is still essentially the narrow-minded academic, resentful of the lack of worldly prestige which his calling traditionally receives, and set on righting the balance in his fantasies.

The speech ends on a more sinister note: the power that Faustus envisages is one which involves military conquest and the invention of strange 'engines for the brunt of war'. It contains elements of destructiveness.

Yet, however analytically critical we might be of Faustus's day-dreams at this point (and I have suggested that the rhythms of the speech encourage empathy rather than analysis) we have to acknowledge that they are hardly evil. Even the war which he dreams of waging – one which will put him on the throne, we notice – will also be, in a sense, a justified one, to free the Netherlands from Spanish and Catholic domination. The average Protestant Englishman or woman in the audience in the 1590s must have had a sneaking sympathy with many of Faustus's desires.

The point, however, must be made that Faustus's ideals are compromised from the start. *Doctor Faustus* is often seen as the story of a man who starts out with high ideals but who, as he is taken over by infernal powers, later degenerates into a mere court entertainer. There is truth in this, but it is not the whole truth. From the very beginning Faustus's aspirations are confused. At times, certainly, they are high-flown and noble-sounding, but at times they make him resemble nothing so much as a cosmic grocer, who will command the powers that inform the universe to 'search all corners of the new-found-world' . . . for what? 'For pleasant fruits'. As it happens, we see Faustus do precisely this in Act IV, when the pregnant Duchess of Vanholt has a craving for grapes. This incident is often cited to show how far Faustus has sunk from his earlier great aspirations, but this is hardly the case: it is what he said he would do in the very beginning.

Valdes and Cornelius
(Act I, Scene 1, ll. 99–165)

Enter Valdes and Cornelius. Who are these two, and what is their function? Certainly they are inventions of Marlowe's own: they do not appear in the German *Faustbuch* or its English translation. For what purpose has Marlowe invented them? We, the audience, know very little about them. According to the scholar in the next scene they are famous necromancers, and Faustus tells us that they have been helping to persuade him to the arts of black magic. But that is about all we ever hear of them. This is their only appearance, and it seems hardly worthwhile considering them as 'characters' in the play at all. Yet they must have a function, surely?

They are not there just so that Faustus has someone to whom he can express his thoughts: his soliloquy has done enough to explain his thought processes, and he even has to repeat himself rather perfunctorily to Valdes and Cornelius in his first address to them. And they, not he, do most of the talking in the rest of the scene. To this extent they seem to be more like figures of temptation from a morality play – but in this case they are rather redundant, for Faustus is already persuaded and needs no further temptation. They do not tell him anything new, and in fact Valdes's first speech seems to be a reprise of many of the things which Faustus has already said in his soliloquy. What, then, is their function in this scene?

I would suggest that their function is twofold: firstly, to continue the vein of language which Faustus has already begun, the language of pleasure projected.

> Faustus, these books, thy wit, and our experience
> Shall make all nations to canonise us.
> As Indian Moors obey their Spanish lords
> So shall the spirits of every element
> Be always serviceable to us three;
> Like lions shall they guard us when we please;
> Like Almaine rutters with their horsemen's staves;
> Or Lapland giants trotting by our sides . . .
> From Venice shall they drag huge argosies,
> And from America the golden fleece,
> That yearly stuffs old Philip's treasury,
> If learned Faustus will be resolute.

This luxurious language is such an important element in the play because it is arguably the case that Faustus, like Valdes here, is more successful at conjuring up pleasure with words than he is at doing it with black magic. The speeches in which Faustus describes what he will do are often genuinely 'magical', creating a poetic reality which Faustus later tries to translate into physical reality. This, then, is the first function of Valdes and Cornelius – to help Faustus to paint his magical picture.

Their second function is, I think, to provide Faustus, albeit momentarily, with some human company on his lonely voyage to damnation. We have already seen that it takes an extraordinarily long time before the play has any real dialogue in it. The first speech is a monologue by the Chorus, then there is Faustus's first long soliloquy, interrupted by a brief command to a servant, then by the Good and Bad Angels, whose speeches hardly comprise 'dialogue', followed by a continuation of the soliloquy. The cumulative effect of this is to create a sense of isolation. Faustus is not really a man in society talking to other men, as characters in dramas usually are. He is a man who is, in a significant way, rather lonely. Later in the play the bulk of Faustus's dialogues will be with the supernatural Mephostophilis. When he meets other humans, he encounters them as spectators of his magic or as victims of his tricks; he hardly even exchanges words with his own servant. The only real exception to this will be the Old Man in the last act.

Thematically, this is effective, for one of the major results of Faustus's power is to distance him from the normal run of humanity. But far though Faustus travels into isolation, there is a moment here when he is still, in a way, a social being. Marlowe has no need to provide Faustus at this point with encouragers or teachers. Faustus could, one gathers, have learnt all his magic from a book, and indeed he seems to do so. But unless the drama of Faustus is to be contained on a totally allegorical level, Marlowe does need to provide him with some human contact. It is not that Valdes and Cornelius should be seen as 'leading Faustus into temptation', or that he should be seen as any less blameworthy because of their 'words having won him' to the study of magic – he himself insists, 'Yet not your words only but mine own fantasy'. It is rather that Faustus, for a brief moment, is shown not to be entirely alone, and not the only man in the world ever to have tried this ultimate experiment.

In the end, of course, Valdes and Cornelius are unimportant. As I say, we never see them again. But momentarily it looks as if they might be Faustus's equals. When Cornelius asks 'Then tell me, Faustus, what shall we three want', it is a shared venture that is being proposed. It does not take long before that is no longer the case: Faustus's conjuring will be in a solitary grove, where he will 'try his cunning by himself'. But at least he celebrates with them a last supper.

Wagner and the scholars
(Act I, Scene 2)

The short exchange between Wagner and the scholars begins a sequence of ironical undercutting which continues throughout *Doctor Faustus*. The scholars question Wagner about Faustus's whereabouts:

1 SCHOLAR: How now sirra, where's thy master?

WAGNER: God in heaven knows.

2 SCHOLAR: Why, dost not thou know then?

WAGNER: Yes, I know, but that follows not.

Wagner's wordplay on 'God in heaven knows' (which foreshadows a later similar pun which Faustus makes on the phrase, 'God forbid', in the last act) is just the first stage of a small rhetorical *tour de force* in which Wagner indulges. Wagner manages to reverse the expected social order: the servant triumphs in wit and logic over the supposedly learned scholars, and triumphs so easily that he can insult them, ignore them, and patronize them at will. A moralistic reading of this scene might point out that because Wagner (as we soon discover) is dabbling, like Faustus, in things he should not, the result is that he is insolent where he should be respectful, and contemptuous where he should be submissive. In performance, however, an audience is hardly likely to respond this way. Wagner's teasing of the scholars is calculated to put us on his side, and to laugh at them as butts of his humour. If the world is being turned upside down, we are invited to enjoy the fact, not to condemn it.

The actual nature of Wagner's victory concerns that which is knowable. Wagner is asked where Faustus is, and presents the scholars with a series of quibbles about the knowability and communicability of that simple 'fact'. The exchange ends with him – having proved that the fact is not definitely knowable in the first place – telling them in the parodied language of the Puritan that Faustus is at dinner. It is a small joke, but its dynamic is important. It concerns the relationship between abstract, theoretical knowledge and plain common sense. Much of the play is about that relationship too.

Raising the devil (1): serious
(Act I, Scene 3)

At this point we run into the textual problems which were discussed in the previous chapter. As has been mentioned, there are two distinct versions of *Doctor Faustus*. In one of them, Faustus's conjuring happens with him on an otherwise empty stage (A-text). In the other (B-text) and in most modern editions, it takes place in the presence of Lucifer himself. The stage direction reads: '*Thunder. Enter* LUCIFER *and four* DEVILS *above.* FAUSTUS *to them, with this speech*'. The play, in effect, splits into two at this point. This problem arises again, with greater consequences, in Act V, and there I will deal with it in greater detail. Here I will just say that I am following the convention of modern editions in general, and that my discussion of this scene is based on the B-text.

Playing the scene with Lucifer and the devils physically onstage eliminates any doubt as to the cosmic significance of Faustus's actions, or to the eventual effectiveness of Faustus's magic: the Devil and his henchmen are seen to be there, already prepared to receive him into their flock. Theatre here returns to its own earliest origins – theatre as ritual.

Indeed, in a parody of the holy ritual with which it had once been associated, the theatre here becomes a place of the enactment of devilish spells.

This is one of the scenes in *Doctor Faustus* where the play loses most in being seen on the page rather than on the stage, in a theatre, in the company of others. For the theatre always has an element of ritual about it. We gather publicly in order to partake of the shared acceptance of a belief that what is going on onstage represents some kind of truth. This is as true for the non-illusionistic stage of Elizabethan London as it is for the most naturalistic drama. And if the ritual works well enough, we may laugh with real pleasure, or cry real tears at the outcome of the ritual.

Or, in the case of *Doctor Faustus*, be genuinely scared. Psychological tests on subjects watching horror movies have shown that the physiological response (heartbeat, sweating, pulse rate) of someone watching something frightening, which they know to be a fiction, does not differ significantly from the physiological response of subjects who are in what they believe to be real danger. The 'magic' of the theatre is that it can also conjure up such effects – and here we have, onstage, in the middle of the ritual that is theatre-going, a man who is himself performing a ritual. No wonder, then, that the following account comes down to us from contemporary sources, of one particularly terrifying Elizabethan performance of *Doctor Faustus*:

Certain players at Exeter acting upon the stage the tragical story of Dr Faustus the conjurer; as a certain number of Devils kept every one his circle there, and as Faustus was busy in his magical invocations, on a sudden they were all dashed, every one harkening other in the ear, for they were all persuaded, there was one devil too many amongst them; and so after a little pause desired the people to pardon them, they could go no further with this matter; the people also understanding the thing as it was, every man hastened to be first out of doors. The players (as I heard it) contrary to their custom spending the night in reading and in prayer got them out of the town the next morning. (Quoted in E. K. Chambers, *The Elizabethan Stage*, p. 423.)

The common-sense barriers between the natural and the supernatural must have seemed terribly frail that night, as the make-believe of *Doctor Faustus* suddenly appeared to be the terrifying reality of an actual demonic manifestation.

I am arguing, of course, for the power of this scene – saying that it is a dramatic moment which should, in its effect on the audience, be genuinely terrifying, as Faustus chants the invocation to Mephostophilis.

The forces which Faustus conjures up are powerful and terrible, and the stage directions, '*Thunder*' and '*Dragon*', unexciting and unimaginative as they look on the page, refer to a theatrical effect which the audience would have found frightening.

When Mephostophilis first appears, Faustus's reaction, too, is one of horror. When Mephostophilis returns in the guise of an old Franciscan friar, Faustus's relief, and ours, should be palpable. It is an almost comic anti-climax. It is also a momentary allowance to Faustus of some of the powers which he claims to command. The greater the tension of the ritual, the greater the relief at its total success; the greater, too, Faustus's achievement seems to be, and the greater the pathos of his eventual fall. And the greater the irony, too; for, lest we forget, the scene begins with Lucifer and the devils appearing above. When do these disappear? Do they stay to the end of the scene? Or do they vanish as the ritual progresses and Mephostophilis materializes? Either way, they exist as a reminder of the reality and the power of the Devil. (The longer they stay there, of course, the greater the sense of the Devil's power will be.) Thus, however great Faustus's power appears to be, it is put into perspective by the presence of Lucifer.

Moreover, while Faustus momentarily congratulates himself on his own power ('Now, Faustus, thou art conjuror laureate: / That canst command great Mephostophilis'), the audience are soon to be disabused. Faustus's first words with Mephostophilis not only set the limits of Faustus's ability to command (Mephostophilis says unequivocally, 'I am a servant to great Lucifer, / And may not follow thee without his leave'), but they also destroy the illusion of Faustus's having conjured up Mephostophilis in the first place:

MEPHOSTOPHILIS: ... I came now hither of mine own accord.

FAUSTUS: Did not my conjuring speeches raise thee? Speak!

MEPHOSTOPHILIS: That was the cause, but yet *per accidens*;
For when we hear one rack the name of God,
Abjure the Scriptures, and his saviour Christ,
We fly in hope to get his glorious soul;

The first great difference between earthly logic and that of hell is being expounded. Faustus believes in a direct chain of cause and effect – 'I summon, he obeys'. The truth (which Faustus stoutly misapprehends, even when it is explained to him) is that Mephostophilis's arrival was not in response to a command, but to an indication of possible gain. He has arrived, not like an obedient servant to his master's call, but like a hunter to the sound of potential prey.

Faustus goes on to speak in words which are, once more, more truthful than he knows, and which the alert reader should spot. He says of himself that,

> This word 'damnation' terrifies not him,
> For he confounds hell in elysium.

The overt meaning – that which Faustus seems to intend to express – is that the Christian hell is no more to be feared than the pagan land of milk and honey, and perhaps that it is no more real. In a similar tone he later says that he thinks hell is just a fable. But there is an ironic undercurrent to the word 'confounds'. Faustus uses it to mean 'makes no distinction between'. But 'confounds' may also mean 'confuses'. Is Faustus here to be seen as confusing heaven and hell? And what about the fact that the word 'confounds' comes so soon after 'this word "damnation"'? For a third meaning of 'confounds' is 'consigns to perdition'.

Immediately, Faustus begins to do what he summoned Mephostophilis for in the first place: to question him about the ultimate secrets of the universe. He starts with the nature of hellish things, and here occurs one of the key interchanges of the play.

FAUSTUS: Where are you damned?

MEPHOSTOPHILIS: In hell.

FAUSTUS: How comes it then that thou art out of hell?

MEPHOSTOPHILIS: Why this is hell, nor am I out of it.
                Think'st thou that I who saw the face of God,
                And tasted the eternal joys of heaven,
                Am not tormented with ten thousand hells,
                In being deprived of everlasting bliss?

If there is one crucial piece of knowledge which Faustus is offered throughout the play, it is this. He learns other things, certainly: details of planetary motion, how to do (or get Mephostophilis to do) various kinds of conjuring tricks. But here, at the very beginning of their conversations together, Mephostophilis offers Faustus the vital truth – that Faustus's own literalism will betray him. For Faustus understands the word 'hell' in its most literal and basic sense – as a *place* in which damned souls reside. Mephostophilis has a more metaphorical understanding of the word: 'Why this is hell, nor am I out of it.' 'This', of course, on one level is not hell at all: it is Faustus's study, and that is all that Faustus can see when he looks around – hence his mocking reply to Mephostophilis. But on another level, Mephostophilis is really, simultaneously, in hell. Once more, hellish logic and earthly logic are shown to operate differently. Faustus, of course, does not believe that Mephostophilis's statement has any truth to it. He probably believes that it is 'just' a figure of speech, a metaphor. But as we shall see, in Mephostophilis's world, figures of speech, images and metaphors can become terrible realities. Faustus's laughing admonition to Mephostophilis to 'Learn . . . of Faustus manly fortitude' seems dreadfully hollow.

Raising the devil (2): parody
(Act I, Scene 4)

And now the tone changes again. Just as there had been a brief comic interlude between Act I, Scene 1 and Act I, Scene 3, so there is here. But Wagner's companion is now the clown (Robin), and far from being light relief, I, 4 is a scene which directly refers to and comments on the one which precedes it. Just as Faustus had conjured up devils, so Wagner conjures up devils; just as Faustus in doing so had found himself a supernatural 'servant' in Mephostophilis, so Wagner now gets himself a servant in the Clown. And just as Faustus had believed himself to have dominion over the powers of hell, so the Clown believes himself to have the strength to kill devils. Both Faustus and the Clown are deluded in these beliefs, but it takes Faustus longer to find this out than it does the Clown. This scene, then, provides a series of parodies of what went on immediately before.

It is a common enough trick to use the grades of society to show the debasement or elevation of an idea. Here, clearly, Faustus's comparatively serious dabbling in demonology, linked as it is with his philosophical inquiries, is here being 'debased' into Wagner's summoning of the malicious devils who beat the Clown. The downward trajectory of the conjuring is going to continue, we discover, for Wagner agrees to teach the Clown 'this conjuring occupation'. It takes no great learning, it seems, to summon the powers of darkness – a fact which corroborates Mephostophilis's claim that it was his 'own accord', not Faustus's skill, which brought him to Faustus.

Doubts
(Act II, Scene 1, ll. 1–29)

By the time we see Faustus again, he is in a very different mood. His first speech, while hardly one of repentance (he promises to 'build an altar and a church [to Beelzebub], / And offer luke-warm blood of new-born babes'), none the less contains a great deal of doubt. Already convinced of his own damnation, he falters in his purpose.

> Now Faustus must thou needs be damned?
> And canst thou not be saved?
> What boots it then to think on God or heaven?
> Away with such vain fancies and despair,
> Despair in God, and trust in Belzebub.
> Now go not backward: no, Faustus, be resolute,
> Why waverest thou? . . .

The tone is precisely that of a man trying to convince himself, and his wavering is the cue for the reappearance of the Good and Bad Angels. Whereas on their previous appearance Faustus had seemed totally oblivious of them, here he appears at least half aware of them: 'O something soundeth in mine ears: / "Abjure this magic, turn to God again",' he tells himself – although he cannot locate precisely where or what this something is. But if he can half hear the Good Angel, he can also half hear the Bad. The Bad Angel's last word echoes in Faustus's head: 'Wealth'. This is what finally turns the scale, banishes his doubts, and leads him to decide that, 'When Mephostophilis shall stand by me, / What God can hurt me?' The logic is unclear – but this is nothing new for Faustus.

Signing the contract
(Act II, Scene 1, ll. 30–75)

Mephostophilis's return heralds the crucial scene in which Faustus literally sells his soul to the devil. Even at this vital moment in the play, when Faustus is challenged to make the great decision, he is still the inveterate questioner, asking Mephostophilis about theology. There is no struggle about the decision itself – it comes easily: 'Ay Mephostophilis, I'll give it thee.' The debate has taken place a few lines earlier. But the dramatic tension of the signing scene is not over yet. Marlowe has shown the worse side of Faustus's nature triumph easily over the better side. He next portrays Faustus beset with external obstacles. To the

47

audience, these are symbols of the rashness of his act. For Faustus himself they are opportunities to turn back.

The first obstacle is that his blood will not flow – a brilliant image which works on the level of matter-of-fact practicality and also at a symbolic level. Practically, of course, it means that he cannot conclude the deal; he has, in effect, run out of ink, and the contract cannot be signed. On another level, though, it has the effect of suggesting a revulsion of nature (both with a capital 'N' and in the sense of Faustus's own 'nature') against the compact with the devil. Nature stops in her course, unwilling to continue her accustomed cycle in the face of Faustus's most unnatural act. And, more obliquely, the ceasing of the flow of blood suggests the death to which Faustus is condemning himself. This level of the action has a wonderful built-in irony: Faustus's blood stops, his circulation stops, in order to give him a chance to save his own 'life'. As soon as his blood flows again, his death-warrant is signed (literally) and his term of twenty-four years begins to tick away. Marlowe generates all these meanings with this stage action, this single image, and he also gives a powerful image of Faustus's own schizophrenia. Faustus's brain and his body, his intellect and his animal functions, are at odds with each other, and the great disassociation has begun.

The devils
(Act II, Scene 1, ll. 76–177)

Devils appear twice in this scene, and both times they do so in order to demonstrate something to Faustus. The first time is in response to Mephostophilis's need to 'fetch him somewhat to delight his mind'. For again, something has happened which appears to threaten Mephostophilis's chances of total success. The inscription which appears on Faustus's arm, '*Homo fuge*', is another ambiguous image. On the one hand it is a warning: 'Fly from what you are doing – desist!' On the other it is a threat: 'Now that you have achieved your aim, fly from the wrath of God!' Faustus himself reads the two possibilities as one when he asks, 'Whither should I fly? / If unto God, he'll throw me down to hell.' Here the objective reality of the image is questioned: Faustus for a moment sees it, then exclaims, 'My senses are deceived, here's nothing writ!' and then changes his mind again: 'O yes, I see it plain.' It is significant that this should come immediately after the signing of the contract, which Faustus believes to be the decisive moment in his career. It is immediately after this that the reality of his sense perceptions becomes uncertain, that he begins either to hallucinate, or not to believe the truth which is in front of him. It is as if, having signed the contract, he is plunged into a world where illusion and reality are uncertain.

The audience is meant to believe that the writing actually exists, and that it is Faustus's now-faulty perception which does not accord it its full status as reality. For it is Mephostophilis who wants him to ignore the writing – hence his need for 'somewhat to delight his mind'. The first show of devils, then, is a deliberate distraction, designed by Mephostophilis to divert Faustus's attention away from a possible message from the heavens.

And here Marlowe's irony works in specifically dramatic terms. The pageant of devils is an illusion which Mephostophilis engineers. An illusion not because the devils are not 'real' – they are, just as Mephostophilis is. But an illusion because they are acting a role in relation to Faustus which is, in the long run, illusory. At the end, he will be torn apart by them, not fêted by them. What they do at this precise moment is *perform* for him – a fact which Faustus himself seems to half realize when, on their exit, he turns to Mephostophilis and asks, 'What means this *show*?' Mephostophilis's answer is significant: 'Nothing, Faustus,' he says, 'but to delight thy mind.' The meaninglessness of Faustus's new powers is already being suggested.

The second appearance of the devils is a visual jest. Whereas the previous show was one of flattery towards Faustus, Faustus here is the victim of a practical joke. Mephostophilis disapproves of Faustus's desire to have a wife – a disapproval which seems based on a misreading of Faustus's exact desires. 'I am,' he says, 'wanton and lascivious, and cannot live without a wife.' He seems to be asking for little more than a sexual companion, but Mephostophilis picks him up on his exact term for what he wants. Mephostophilis disapproves because the word 'wife' implies the sanctification of a relationship by holy matrimony. Finding Faustus obstinate, Mephostophilis provides a demonic parody of what he desires – '*a* DEVIL *dressed like a woman, with fireworks*'.

There are two points to make about this. Firstly, that the image can be played in a horrific way as well as a comic one. It must be repeated that stage directions on the page can often seem silly, whereas on the stage, the action they refer to may well be extremely powerful. This is particularly true of special effects. '*A* DEVIL *dressed like a woman, with fireworks*': we should try to make an imaginative leap back to Marlowe's stage and try to conjecture how this might have been performed. For example, the devil dressed like a woman: is this a direction for something like a pantomime dame, an easily recognizable comic caricature? Or is it a direction to the actors for something more subtle? There would, of course, have been no actresses on the stage in Marlowe's theatre; every part in the play would have been taken by a male actor, even the immortal Helen. So the appearance of a woman on the stage was an illusion in any case. Indeed, for a few moments it might not be evident that it was a devil at all, so that only after the audience has been lulled into believing that Mephostophilis has agreed to Faustus's demand does its demonic nature become clear. And then the fireworks: a powerful and probably unexpected device on Marlowe's stage, and one which can shock an audience with noise, startle them with colour, and which leaves the sulphurous smell of cordite lingering in the air: a fine emblem for hell.

It should be remembered that the overall effect is to be considered as much as the means for achieving that effect. Did Marlowe want a sudden joke? A shock? To scare the audience? To amuse it? Perhaps a combination of these – but quite how much of each remains a problem for each and every director in each and every production. Richard Burton, in his film of *Doctor Faustus*, tackled this scene in a way which could only be done on film. He showed Faustus embracing a beautiful young woman, who then turned into an ugly and deformed crone. The technique has been used in dozens of horror movies, but it still retains its force as a symbol of corruption. In using this image, Burton found a contemporary equivalent for Marlowe's fireworks – one which worked through horror and repulsion rather than through laughter.

I will admit that I have a preference for a comic way of playing this scene, since to allow it the 'low humour' of a practical joke shows that Mephostophilis is not above such things. Much has been made – especially by critics arguing for the unity of the play – of the thematic importance of some of the later farcical scenes. It is, however, salutary to see that in this earlier stage of the play Mephostophilis himself is quite capable of the occasional 'mere conjuring trick'.

The second point about this short stage image is that, however one plays it, and whatever weight one gives the potentially sombre side of the image, one thing is certain: that what we are seeing is Faustus's first attempt, after the signing of the contract, to command Mephostophilis to 'do for him, and bring him whatsoever', and that it goes badly wrong for Faustus. His powers are, as ever, less than he believed, and Mephostophilis's capability to redefine the terms of the agreement is undiminished.

The final image of this scene has an element of pathos about it. The deal is concluded and the bargain agreed. Faustus, the power-seeker, diverted by Mephostophilis from his desire for a wife, is offered the secrets of the universe. The books which Mephostophilis hands him are symbols of this. The disparity between expectation and achievement fuels this image. Faustus the scholar has sold his soul – for a few books! The bathos of this image is not played up; Faustus is clearly pleased with his new toy. But the audience is left with an image of power and knowledge which, far from being exotically occult, is rather mundane – the books themselves. Faustus, after all, already has a collection of necromantic books, one of which enabled him to 'summon' Mephostophilis. However, we know that such books have little power in themselves – Mephostophilis came in order to gain Faustus's soul, not because the book's spells forced him to. Perhaps, it is true, the ones which Mephostophilis is giving him are different in kind, more powerful. And yet the image seems to indicate that he is being given nothing really new.

Apart from magic, the books contain information about 'all characters and planets of the heavens' and 'all plants, herbs and trees that grow upon the earth'. Faustus's soul is being sold for a reference library! But this was the point from which Faustus started out in his first soliloquy. The scholar, already the master of so much knowledge, thirsts for more. And in this first flush of success, Faustus's new books delight him. It is not until the next scene that Faustus shows any dissatisfaction with the kind of knowledge which Mephostophilis has to offer. Then, as Mephostophilis instructs him in astronomy, Faustus exclaims bad-temperedly, 'These slender questions Wagner can decide.' Which is true.

Faustus wavers
(Act II, Scene 2)

The general impression of the first half of Act II, Scene 2 is of a single image, the image of Faustus standing on the edge of perdition, deciding how to react. The previous scene had begun with Faustus in a mood of momentary repentance, or at least a mood in which he was arguing with himself about his situation. Act II, Scene 2 also opens with Faustus repenting his former rashness. Here, though, his rebellion against the devil has greater strength. Faustus even, astonishingly, wins a round in the verbal battle with Mephostophilis. Admittedly, Faustus's first assault on Mephostophilis is unlikely to impress an audience.

> When I behold the heavens then I repent,
> And curse thee wicked Mephostophilis,
> Because thou hast deprived me of those joys.

The sincerity of the regret is not to be questioned, but Faustus's eagerness to blame it all on Mephostophilis does not ring true. When Mephostophilis replies, '`Twas thine own seeking, Faustus, thank thyself,' we are inclined to agree with him rather than with Faustus. (Later on in the play, he will be more willing to take the credit for Faustus's downfall.)

But Mephostophilis overplays his hand and, engaging in logical quips with Faustus, he unintentionally leads Faustus into a position of orthodox faith. Attempting to prove that heaven is not so desirable, Mephostophilis says that heaven 'was made for man; then he's more excellent'. Mephostophilis's tactics are bad here. He is making a mistake which he will not repeat, of trying to prove logically the validity of his own position. In doing so, he engages in precisely the kind of casuistry which Faustus believes himself to be so proficient in. For Faustus, in the early part of this play, is portrayed as the ultimate sceptical reasoner. Given any position, Faustus will attempt to prove the opposite. He will prove that law, medicine, philosophy and theology are worthless, will prove that hell is a fable, that the afterlife is a trifle and so on. So as soon as Mephostophilis attempts to prove that 'heaven ... is not half so fair / As ... any man that breathes on earth', Faustus's inevitable response is to find a counter-argument. In this case it is an orthodox, but powerful one –

> If heaven was made for man, 'twas made for me:
> I will renounce this magic and repent.

– and Faustus's word 'repent' cues the appearance of the Good Angel, in a reversal of Mephostophilis's original appearance in Act I, Scene 3. Mephostophilis, we remember, had originally appeared because, 'when we hear one rack the name of God ... / We fly in hope to get his glorious soul.' Here it is the Good Angel who appears at the moment of Faustus's decision to repent, as if conjured by Faustus's words.

The stage relationship between Faustus and the Good and Bad Angels continues to develop. Here, more than elsewhere, they seem to be an emblem of what goes on inside Faustus's mind. They seem to dramatize rather than to instigate the shift which takes place in Faustus between line 11 ('I will renounce this magic and repent') and line 18 ('My heart's so hardened I cannot repent'). Even here, though, they are not merely projections of Faustus's own mind: they are also things external to him which buzz in his ears that he is a spirit.

But what is made abundantly clear in this exchange is that the ball is now in Faustus's court, and that the ability to repent is the key to his salvation. The external actions which he has so far performed are comparatively meaningless. Even the signing of the contract with the devil is by no means an insuperable obstacle. The Good Angel states the case succinctly: 'Faustus repent, yet God will pity thee.' The Bad Angel's attempt to argue that Faustus is already a spirit and therefore beyond redemption should certainly be seen as a trap, and Faustus, still energetically rebelling against the voices of hell, will have none of it. What is at stake is the inward state of Faustus's mind, which might make repentance a real possibility.

However, just at the point when the debate seems to be in full swing, the attempted rebellion collapses again – cued, not by logic or argument, but by assertion. The Bad Angel simply states, or predicts, that 'Faustus never shall repent', and leaves the stage. Faustus, left without the Bad Angel to argue against, promptly gives up the struggle and swings to the opposite pole, with, 'My heart's so hardened I cannot repent!' This is a somewhat enigmatic line. For a start, it is not strictly true: he has already shown that he can and does repent whenever he beholds the heavens. Presumably we are to read his assertion as meaning that he cannot fully repent, that he cannot stay repentant, or that he cannot bring himself to give up all that he has seemed to gain by his contract with the devil. We should bear in mind when considering those moments when Faustus is urged to repent, or when he attempts to repent, that the word means more than just 'regret'. An Elizabethan Christian would have thought of repentance as quite a complex process, involving the acknowledgement of a sin, the confession of the sin before God, the affirmation of faith in God's mercy (his ability and willingness to forgive the sin), and also the amendment of the ways of the sinner thereafter. We are often shown Faustus beginning this process of repentance, but he is never able to complete it.

But what prevents him from completing it? Faustus himself says it is his own hardness of heart, but that is hardly an illuminating phrase. It does not explain very much, and does not even seem true. Certainly this soliloquy does not seem to be that of a hard-hearted man. In fact, what prevents Faustus from fully repenting seems to be more in the way of fear.

There is an opposition set up within the play between two attitudes to human destiny. The position which the Good Angel offers is one which stresses the supremacy of individual freedom of choice; the Good Angel's essential message is that Faustus has only to choose, fully to choose, repentance, and the way is open to him. What Faustus's own speech dramatizes, however, is a position in which freedom of choice seems completely circumscribed:

> Scarce can I name salvation, faith, or heaven,
> But fearful echoes thunders in mine ears,

> 'Faustus, thou art damned': Then swords and knives,
> Poison, guns, halters and envenomed steel
> Are laid before me to dispatch myself:

Faustus, it seems, is subject to a reality which blots out the free play of choice which the Good Angel announces. He believes in his heart of hearts what the Bad Angel says – that he is already damned. His only choices at that point are to continue in his damnation, or to give in to the 'swords and knives', which he knows well to be laid before him by the devil, and to do away with himself – thus committing a mortal sin which would ensure his damnation as certainly as the contract with the devil would. From the point of view of the Good Angel, Faustus has freedom of choice. From Faustus's own position, though, the only choices which he appears to have are between damnation and damnation, since the very naming of salvation induces in him a state of despair which is suicidal.

Once more, as readers and audience, we are confronted with an image whose location on the scale of literalism and metaphor is problematic. On the one hand, we can read this as a literal depiction of Faustus's situation – that the devil comes to him, takes over his mind, and lays before him the instruments of suicide. On another level, Marlowe is here producing a powerful symbol of a psychological state, a state of despair which is so deep that the very attempt to escape from it redoubles its intensity.

It should be remembered that the advocate of freedom of choice is the Good Angel; as such, what he offers is, we presume, true, and the ultimate reality of Faustus's situation according to cosmic law is that he can indeed repent, that it is not too late, and that, according to the rules of the game, his options are still open. But what prevents this is his own deep conviction (embodied in the apparitions of the swords and knives) that this is not so and that he is already damned. It is part of Faustus's predicament that he mistakes his own subjective feelings (the feeling that he is already damned) for the total truth about his situation. But it is psychologically convincing that this very belief is what prevents him from making the effort of will which the Good Angel is urging him to make. It is, in theological terms, the very problem of faith itself. In psychological terms, it is as if a man were being told, 'If you only believe this to be true, it will be true,' and the man replies, 'But I cannot believe it.'

On the one level, this is a dramatization of Faustus's own specific situation. On another level it is the dramatization of the fears of a culture. Two opposing models of Christianity were fighting for supremacy during the sixteenth century. In one – the more orthodox, broad Protestant and Catholic model – salvation could be attained through a combination of the efforts of the individual, and the grace and mercy of God towards that individual. It is this attaining of salvation which is dramatized by most sixteenth-century morality plays. But an opposing model, which was increasingly influential, asserted that individual efforts held no place in the scheme of things. John Calvin, the Puritan theologian, in his *Institutes of the Christian Religion*, argued that each man, woman and child has been marked down for salvation or damnation from the first day of creation, and that nothing anybody does will alter that. Calvin goes on to assert that 'This plan was founded upon his freely given mercy, without regard to human worth; but by his just and irreprehensible but incomprehensible judgement he has barred the door of life to those whom he has given over to damnation.' (Calvin, II, 931)

The Good Angel's cosmology is the traditional one. Faustus, on the other hand, tends towards a belief in some sort of doctrine of election or predestination. It was this which informed his distortion of biblical quotations into 'What will be, shall be', in his first soliloquy, and it is this which, in part, is now responsible for his conviction that he is irrevocably damned. The debate is never fully articulated in terms of Calvinism, and it would be taking it too far to suggest that Marlowe's play is 'about' the conflict between the Calvinist doctrine of election and the more traditional view of salvation through faith, good works and individual repentance. However, to an audience for whom this issue was a live one, it must have been significant that the traditional view was spoken by an agent of heaven, the Good Angel, and that it was the deceived Faustus who returned time after time to the idea of the impossibility of repentance.

It must be stressed that Faustus's position is not that of a thoroughgoing Calvinist, although it is not irreconcilable with that. A convinced Calvinist would not date his damnation, as Faustus does, from the time of an individual action such as signing the contract, but would see it as having been written in the book of creation from the very dawning of time. Yet, as I say, the two positions are not so very far apart, for the believer in election sees proof of his beliefs in the actions of men and women. Thus, to a Calvinist, Faustus is damned, not because he signs the contract, but because it was his original destiny to be damned. The signing of the contract would merely be an outward and visible sign of the fact that he was originally scheduled for damnation. It would, in effect, simply prove the Calvinist point.

The issue of Calvinism is more complex than this, and contains difficulties which cannot be gone into here. To sum up, however, let me
repeat the basic point that the Good Angel, who is the dramatic representative of God's truth, puts forward the possibility of repentance time
after time. Faustus rejects this possibility because of his own deep conviction that he is already damned – and thus, in the end, he really is
damned. One might think of this as the acting-out of a theological truth.
In a larger sense, though, the truth which it enacts is a psychological
one.

The key word in all of this is one which belongs both to the theological
vocabulary and, by implication, to the psychological one: it is 'despair'.
According to traditional Christian morality, despair is, paradoxically, a
form of pride. Certainly, in the character of Faustus, we see how the two
are related. When Faustus talks of the temptations to suicide which have
been laid before him, he admits that, 'long ere this I should have done
the deed, / Had not sweet pleasure conquered deep despair.' This pairing
of opposites is important, reminding us that the Faustus that we see
between the signing of the contract and the termination of the term of
his mortality is anything but blind to his peril. Deep despair, it is suggested here, is his normal state, tempered only by sweet pleasure. His
new state is one of extremes. And as he conjures up the pictures of sweet
pleasures with his words, the despair turns into a grim resolution, and 'I
cannot repent' becomes the more defiant 'Faustus *shall* not repent.'

So he turns brusquely to Mephostophilis, to 'dispute again, / And
reason of divine astrology' (notice the irony of the word 'divine', which
has surreptitiously crept into his speech). The demand seems to be expressing a need for something more to 'delight [his] mind', for some sweet
pleasure to divert him from his deep despair. It is a recurrent pattern: as
soon as Faustus thinks seriously about his situation, he is offered something to divert him from such thoughts. In this instance, Mephostophilis
does not have to force the issue. Faustus himself demands diversion.

But this next debate with Mephostophilis does not satisfy him, for
once more Faustus is being told something which he more or less knows.
A few details he might have been in doubt about, but what Mephostophilis presents him with is in most aspects the familiar Universe of the
fifteenth- and sixteenth-century pre-Copernican scientist. There are no
great revelations here, only a confirmation of an already-existing world
view. As Faustus says, 'Who knows not the double motion of the
planets?' It is all rather an anti-climax.

This very anti-climax, however, leads Faustus on to the crucial question, 'Now tell me who made the world?' Mephostophilis's answer is yet

another example of Faustus learning what he already knows. This time, however, it happens obliquely, since Mephostophilis will not give a direct answer, but Faustus is left in no doubt as to what the answer is. This accomplishes the final twist, taking Faustus full circle. He had started the scene proclaiming, 'When I behold the heavens then I repent'. Now he is back to that state: 'Think, Faustus, upon God, that made the world.' Once more, his words cue in the Angels. Faustus's 'Is't not too late?' elicits the echoing, 'Too late', from the Bad Angel. Once more the Angels seem to be acting out the turmoil in Faustus's mind. But this time the Good Angel wins the debate, and Faustus is tipped over into a genuinely contrite prayer.

It is in this scene that the peculiarity of the nature of the relationship between morality play and tragedy is made most apparent. The scene up to this point has been essentially one from a tragedy: a protagonist, on the brink of a fatal decision, comes close to drawing back. The predominant dramatic tone is one of psychological realism; the character's backings-and-forwardings are motivated by specifics in the text, and even if there is one Good and one Bad Angel on the stage at the same time as the main character, the things they say could almost have been said by the protagonist in soliloquy. The scene, apart from their presence and the fact that we know one of the two main characters to be a demon from hell, is as 'realistic' as any in a Shakespearean tragedy, and as focused on the psychological interest of an individual under stress as a soliloquy in *Hamlet*. The entrance of Lucifer, however, changes all that.

To put Lucifer on the stage is different from putting on Mephostophilis. The latter is an agent of hell, certainly, but one in recognizably human form, and a lesser dignitary in the ranks of the infernal. Lucifer is the Devil himself, and his stage portrayal is a parody of portrayals of God in medieval mystery plays. The play is immediately transformed from the tragedy of the individual to medieval holy drama – the drama of ritual once more. And, as if Lucifer's own presence were not enough, the scene continues in another kind of parody: the parody of the morality play and the pageant of the Seven Deadly Sins.

As the play turns from tragedy to morality, Faustus turns from free agent to subject of the Devil. In the presence of Lucifer there is no possibility of the free debate of the intellect which Faustus had managed to sustain earlier in the scene, even in the presence of Mephostophilis. Faustus is no longer centre stage – the Prince of Darkness dominates, and the interest in psychology is dropped. What takes its place is a parodic enactment of a Puritan's worst fears about the dangers of the stage, for here (as in Act II, Scene 1) Faustus is led towards perdition by means of a performance.

Faustus watches the pageant of the Seven Deadly Sins as if it were a play put on for his private benefit – which, in a way, it is. It is a replay of the old moralities, but done 'for real', stage-managed by the Devil himself, and having the express intention of ensuring a soul's damnation rather than of celebrating its salvation. Faustus becomes a slightly rowdy and interruptive audience to this play, and instead of being the central protagonist of his own tragedy, he is re-cast momentarily as the observer of this Devil's morality play. His responses, moreover, are couched in terms which are exclusively aesthetic: 'That sight will be as pleasing unto me as Paradise was to Adam the first day of his creation' (another singularly inappropriate phrase); Faustus is presented with the emblematic representations of all things unattractive, and his response is pleasure at the representation rather than disgust at the things represented. Marlowe shows Faustus here as the naïve spectator, able to respond to the surface level of the entertainment, but unable to grasp the deeper significance of it. This, of course, is precisely what the Devil wants. It is not any kind of rational argument or logic which effects the transition of Faustus from penitent back to devil-worshipper: rather it is the shift in theatrical genre. The power of the Devil lies in the fact that he can decide what sort of play Faustus is in, he can write the script himself, and can assign Faustus his role in it.

After the pageant of the Seven Deadly Sins, Faustus is promised a visit to hell itself, 'at midnight'. We never hear again about this incident, and are left to wonder why Marlowe included it. Was Faustus to be shown the reality of hell? Or another false picture of 'all manner of delight'? Does it mitigate his obstinacy, or does it make us even more amazed at his refusal or inability to repent? My own belief is that Faustus is to be shown another form of diversionary 'delight' – in other words, it is a trick. But by the end of this scene, Faustus is safely of the Devil's party once more.

We should note Lucifer's parting-gift to him: another book! Books are constant and essential props in *Doctor Faustus*. They are the tools of Faustus's trade and the symbols of his magic. He is by upbringing a man of books: he begins the play by perusing them, continues by choosing his necromantic books, and he receives gifts of books from Mephostophilis and from Lucifer himself. He sets great store by them, for they are part of his own sense of his power. The critic Harry Levin has noted that the historical conjuror Faustus was originally called Georg, and that 'he lost his original Christian name and got another by being confounded with

Johan Fust, one of the earliest printers' (*The Overreacher*, p. 109). If this is true it is a delightful accident, and one which ties in with the main themes of *Doctor Faustus*. In the play it is specifically the 'necromantic books' which are dangerous; yet it is possible to see in Marlowe's story part of the Renaissance ambivalence towards learning itself. The massive explosion of all kinds of knowledge, which the growth of literacy and the expansion of the printing trade were doing so much to foster, made learning seem, to some people, a dangerous thing in itself.

Robin and the book
(Act II, Scene 3)

The theme of books and their powers continues in Act II, Scene 3, the second of the low-life conjuring scenes. There is some debate as to whether this Clown (now called Robin) is the same character as the Clown in Act I, Scene 4. Critics who believe them to be two different characters point out that the Clown in the earlier scene is a simpleton and a butt, unlike the domineering Robin of this scene. This argument is based on false logic, however. The Clown of Act I, Scene 4 was in the presence of his social and intellectual superior, the well-read and witty Wagner; now, in Act II, Scene 3, he takes the opportunity to play high-status, and he attempts to lord it over the less impressive Dick. What we see in this scene is an example of the venerable comic tradition of a hierarchy of relationships, in which a character who is bossed around at one point in the play reappears later, dominating some other poor unfortunate. The effect is to show the rot spreading further and further down the social scale, from Faustus to Wagner to Robin to Dick.

Robin, we learn, has stolen one of Faustus's books. Robin and Dick make jokes about each other's illiteracy, and it is this illiteracy which now prevents them from making anything of the book. Instead, they go off to the tavern in pursuit of something to drink. Their technique for avoiding payment for it looks as though it will owe more to the traditions of vagabond literature (such as the 'coney-catching' treatises describing the tricks of rogues and thieves) than it will to the powers of darkness.

The parody of conjuring, then, is suggested in this scene, but never fully articulated. It collapses instead into a demonstration of the Clown's inability to manipulate the magic, and contains a suggestion that the more basic appetites of Robin and Dick might make for a (temporary) defence against the perils into which Faustus is being led.

Chorus 1

Up to this point, the physical action of the play has been contained within a comparatively small compass – mainly in and around Faustus's study. The first Chorus serves to break up this claustrophobic setting, and to move the action onto a larger scale, taking Faustus, in the imagination of the audience, to 'Olympus' top', allowing him to view 'the clouds, the planets, and the stars' and to 'prove cosmography, / That measures coasts and kingdoms of the earth'.

For the first time, that is, Faustus's magic really seems to take off. We have not, after all, seen him *do* very much magic up to this point; rather, we have seen magic done to him. In dealing with the idea of magic on stage, a playwright has, effectively, three options open to him. Magic can be represented by special effects, such as those used by a stage conjuror. Or he can use the 'magic' of language – the deceptive ability of the poet to conjure up for an audience things which are not really there. Or he can use the magic of stage convention; closely related to the magic of language, this relies upon the 'suspension of disbelief' which enables an audience to believe in things which it knows to be untrue. All of these kinds of magic are used in this middle part of the play. Stage conventions create the magical effect of Faustus's invisibility in Act III, Scene 2, just as a simple costume change creates the effect of meta-morphosis into cardinals in Act III, Scene 1. The Chorus's speech, how-ever, is an example of the former kind of magic, the magic of language, which 'transports' the audience, just as Faustus is meant to be trans-ported. Earlier in the play we have seen Faustus conjuring up for himself, through language, the delights of necromantic power, but here the Chorus takes over a part of that function. The Chorus here does not speak, as he did in the prologue and will in the epilogue, in a moralizing voice. On the contrary, he now seems to be conspiring with Faustus, and participating in his pleasures. He will do the same in his next appear-ance, when he tells us of Faustus's travels to the Emperor's court. In fact, it seems that the voice of the Chorus itself may be divided into two components, a little like the Good and Bad Angels. The Chorus of the prologue and epilogue moralizes about Faustus's downfall, but the Chorus in the middle of the play seems to take part in the pleasure, and to identify himself with Faustus.

The effect here of having the previously disapproving Chorus tell us almost enthusiastically about Faustus's feats, is to change (once more) our focus on Faustus. We are entering the part of the play when Faustus will be seen as the instigator of actions, as a successful trickster, and even, in a strange way, as a kind of anti-Catholic champion. It is an interesting shift, for although Faustus dominates the stage in Acts III and IV, the action over which he presides is less weighty. These two acts are filled with practical jokes and farcical routines, and are comparatively lacking in the more complex arguments and ironies which predominated in Acts I and II, and which will re-surface in Act V. It is this change in mood which has occasioned much critical debate as to what part Marlowe himself played in the authorship of these scenes.

In fact, in Acts III and IV, stage image predominates over word – a fact which means that these two acts often make poor reading but excellent theatre. It has sometimes been held that the comic and farcical scenes in this part of *Doctor Faustus* are blemishes on the play – another reason why admirers of Marlowe often prefer to assign them to someone else! However, there is also a strong critical tradition, with which I am in sympathy, which maintains that whoever wrote them, the comic scenes are an essential element in the overall power of *Doctor Faustus*.

The Vatican
(Act III, Scenes 1 and 2)

Certainly, the scenes in the Vatican do not represent a mere diversion. The picture is a carefully balanced one. Faustus and Mephostophilis are of the Devil's party, and Marlowe needs to show this. But he needs, too, to keep the audience at least partially on Faustus's side. The solution is brilliant in its economy: Faustus is shown playing devilish and blasphemous tricks – but he plays them on the Pope! To an English Protestant audience in the late sixteenth century, of course, the Pope was a kind of Antichrist. So Marlowe gets to have his cake and eat it too. Faustus's ungodliness is shown, but in such a way as to keep the audience cheering for him. Indeed, Marlowe all but has Faustus strike an explicit blow for the Protestant cause. The particular case in which he interferes involves 'Saxon Bruno' and a debate about the proper extent of papal power. Bruno has been set up as a rival pontiff by the German Emperor, a fact which is enough to condemn them both, in the eyes of the Vatican, as 'lollards and bold schismatics' – i.e., Protestant heretics. The freeing of Bruno is presented as a heroic act, one which is in the tradition of anti-clerical satire, and the Pope is portrayed as proud, wrathful and gluttonous – almost a compendium of the Deadly Sins which we saw in Act II, Scene 2. The actual rescue is done comically, with Faustus and Mephostophilis disguised as cardinals: it is a jest-book scene. But there is an irony here. Faustus's original conjuring of Mephostophilis stipulated that he should return as a Franciscan friar, in which guise he has presumably appeared on stage throughout. Here Mephostophilis has changed his disguise – but Faustus is now also in the guise of a Catholic clergyman. As an image on stage, this cannot but link Faustus more and more inextricably in the audience's mind with Mephostophilis: on stage they now even look alike.

This idea of linking through theatrical images may be taken even further. Most Elizabethan stages had a gallery above, which was part of the playing area. This would be a logical place for Faustus and Mephostophilis to stand and watch the action during the earlier part of this scene, before they come down and join in the fun. According to Mephostophilis, they are in his privy chamber, whereas the confrontation between Bruno and the Pope clearly takes place in a more public area. It is reasonable to conclude, then, that they are literally standing in a different part of the stage from the Pope and his court, and the gallery would be a logical choice, suggesting, as it could, a separate room. But this strengthens the impression of Faustus's being allied with the forces of hell, since the gallery is where Lucifer and the four devils must have stood in Act I, Scene 3, when they are described as being 'above'. The stage becomes, in part at least, a moral diagram, and the stage position of characters can tell the audience a great deal about their function. If this sounds implausibly untheatrical, note that the same theatrical 'code' continues today, and is easily understood even by very small children: when, in a pantomime, the Good Fairy appears, she tends to do so from a special place that is understood to be 'hers'; King Rat (or whoever) appears from a different place – perhaps from underneath the stage or from the opposite side. Good Fairies and King Rats, of course, are indirect descendants of morality-play characters, such as the Good and Bad Angels, and the morality-play elements of *Doctor Faustus* invite this kind of spatial interpretation.

The second Vatican scene (Act III, Scene 2) shows Marlowe playing variations on his use of the stage. Here the action does descend to the level of farce – although 'descend' is too dismissive a word for what happens. The farce is very good farce, and depends upon the visual convention of the audience being able to see what the majority of characters on the stage cannot – the 'invisible' Faustus. Faustus's tricks are petty, of course, but they serve also to show up the pettiness of the papal court. Or rather, they show the ease with which God's deputy here on earth can be transformed from his rather pompous dignity to the gross indignity of the man shouting at his cardinals, 'Ye lubbers, look about'. The solemnity of the ritual cursing, too, is undercut by the actual words of the curse:

> Cursed be he that stole his Holiness' meat from the table.
> *Maledicat Dominus* . . .
> Cursed be he that struck Friar Sandelo a blow on the pate.
> *Maledicat Dominus*.

The rituals of heaven and hell are degraded to petty revenges for indignities suffered. And, more important, they are powerless. Faustus cannot be cursed to hell by the Pope or his friars: he already knows that he is going there.

Even in a modern staging, without the topical immediacy of the anti-Catholic satire, this comes across as a beautifully written comic scene, and one which is composed with the art of the comedian in mind. The spring is wound up as Faustus and Mephostophilis become invisible; thereafter they can play whatever visual tricks they wish on the main action, upstaging, mirroring, parodying and disturbing that action as they please. They watch the consequences of the previous scene, in which Faustus and Mephostophilis spirited Bruno away. And these consequences are in themselves comic, since the audience knows the reason for the difference between the two parties' understanding of events, and knows that there is no way in which the cardinals will be able to explain their position to the Pope. Faustus, invisible, disturbs the Vatican's routine by snatching food; the proud, gluttonous, pompous Pope is humiliated repeatedly; the slightly ludicrous ritual of bell, book and candle is performed, and then that, too, is interrupted as Faustus and Mephostophilis '*beat the* FRIARS, *fling fireworks among them, and Exeunt*'. The rhythm of the scene, the use of different levels of 'information' of stage action, the varying of pace, the repetition with variation – all these are signs of a very accomplished comic writer at work.

One wonders, though, if laughter was the only response to this scene by Marlowe's original audience. I have argued that the Pope is a bogyman for the Elizabethan English audience, and that the Vatican, Catholicism in general and the Pope in particular, are legitimate targets for satire. Yet might there not have been a little fear mixed in with the audience's laughter? The Pope, for all his wrong-headedness, must surely represent a kind of spiritual power which is recognized as Christian. And Faustus triumphs over him so easily. The helplessness of the Christian representative in the play – the most powerful Christian on earth – must, even to good Protestants, have caused a minor *frisson* of fear. If Faustus's power is sometimes portrayed frivolously, it is not shown as negligible.

The trick on the Vintner and a time-warp
(Act III, Scene 3)

The scene in which Robin and Dick attempt to steal the Vintner's cup
seems simple enough, and in many ways it is. It does, however, raise an
interesting question: when does it actually happen?

The scene is clearly a continuation of the episode in Act II in which
Robin offers to stand Dick a drink and 'not pay one penny for it'. His
method of not paying for it is to steal a valuable cup from the alehouse,
and the action of this scene seems therefore to take place only a few
hours after the action of Act II, Scene 3. But if this is the case, the scene
logically belongs rather earlier in the play – soon after Act II, Scene 3, in
fact. After all, a great deal of time has elapsed between then and the end
of the Vatican sequence. Faustus, the Chorus told us, spent eight days
touring Mount Olympus and travelling round the world, then he rested
a short while at home, then he went to Rome, a trip which we have seen
take at least two days. It is a strange way of telling the story, to focus on
Faustus, and then to leap back ten days or more in order to complete
the alehouse story.

Things get even more confused when Mephostophilis enters the scene.
He has been brought, he says, 'From Constantinople'. When he exits at
the end of the scene, he tells us he is going to 'the Great Turk's Court'
(presumably Constantinople again) to rejoin Faustus. Does that mean,
then, that the alehouse scene is taking place *during* the round-the-world
trip which Faustus takes before he goes to Rome? Possibly, but the
Chorus did not suggest, in describing that voyage, that Faustus stopped
off at courts along the way: he seemed then to be on a lonely scientific
voyage of discovery. However, in the *next* speech which the Chorus has,
at the beginning of Act IV, we are told that *after* the Vatican escapade,
Faustus visited 'royal courts of Kings'. According to Mephostophilis,
then, the most likely time for the alehouse episode to be happening is
after the visit to Rome. This has the effect of restoring the dramatic
coherence of the order of scenes (if Robin and Dick stole the cup after
the Vatican adventure, then the scene is in the 'right' place in the play),
but then we have to imagine that either this is a different visit to the
alehouse from the one in Act II, Scene 3, which makes for bad comic
plotting, or else that they've been in the alehouse for nearly two weeks,
which makes for a terrible hangover!

Either way, there is an oddity in the time-scale here. It is not a major
interpretative problem in the play, of course, and perhaps it seems foolish
to labour the point, but it is something which I want to raise, largely in
order to consider some of the possible explanations for it.

One explanation might be that the whole thing is irrelevant, and that I am making far too much of it; that all Marlowe was doing was making use of the dramatic convention which allows a playwright to say, in effect, 'Meanwhile . . .' Admittedly, it is quite a big 'meanwhile', but that should not bother the reader unduly. Thus, the time element is of no real significance. This is a perfectly plausible explanation – although there are too many references to time and place in both the Chorus's speeches and in the alehouse scene for me to feel totally convinced by it. If Marlowe had not wanted the audience to bother about exactly *when* things were happening, why did he give figures like 'eight days'?

Secondly, the discrepancy can be explained by referring to the whole problem of authorship. It may be argued that the confusion arises because Marlowe is writing one set of lines (e.g., the Chorus's) and another unidentified writer is penning the comic scenes, and was not careful enough to tie his story-line in with Marlowe's. Again, this is perfectly plausible. It fits in with much scholarly opinion on the composition of the play, and indeed it sounds quite likely: writing by committee is quite likely to produce some mis-matches, and since nobody's enjoyment of the piece is going to be too hampered by the discrepancy, it can safely be ignored. Again, though, the argument is basically that the time-scale simply is not important.

My resistance to the two explanations offered above lies in the fact that the time-warp effect which is experienced if one *does* pay attention to the time-scale, seems so *right*. Whether it came about by accident or design, it is dramatically totally appropriate that Faustus and Mephostophilis should operate on a time-scale which is different from that of the real world, that time should take on a relativistic quality for them, and that they should seem to be outside the kinds of temporal rules which govern the rest of humanity. The distortion of time occurs elsewhere in the play – notably in Faustus's last soliloquy. It makes perfect dramatic sense that distortion should take place here.

It is also the case that thematically this is exactly the right place in the play for this scene, since the action, once more, directly parodies what has gone before. Faustus's supernatural thieving from the banquet of the Pope becomes Robin's more down-to-earth theft of a goblet from a tavern. Robin and Dick's attempts to conceal the cup from the luckless Vintner (who, incidentally, comes across as a much more dignified figure than the Pope) lead them into an attempt to impress him with their conjuring. Robin, it seems, has been putting in some work on the text, and can now successfully pronounce the words which eluded him in Act II, Scene 3: 'O, Demogorgon, Belcher and Mephostophilis'.

Mephostophilis now appears in the scene, in the unusual role of the agent of poetic justice: the thieves are punished by him, although not for their original crime, but for their impudence in attempting to summon him. If the stealing of the cup presents a parallel to Faustus's stealing of the Pope's meat and drink, the punishment of Robin and Dick for their fumbling attempts at sorcery foreshadows the greater and more protracted punishment of Faustus for his devilish practices.

Act IV: the problems

Act IV of *Doctor Faustus* has been much reviled. It is here, we are often told, that we see the worst results of writing by committee. Whoever wrote these scenes – and many Marlowe critics are quite certain that it was not Marlowe himself – they made a poor job of it. This act comprises little more than a series of stories adapted in a slipshod way from the original prose *Historie of the Damnable Life and Deserved Death of Doctor John Faustus*, presented as low farce in order to gratify the debased taste of the unsophisticated groundlings. As an audience, the best we can do is sit through them patiently and wait for Act V, where the play becomes great drama again. (Unless, that is, we have the good luck to be watching a production in which the director has had the taste to cut them out altogether.)

That is one extreme. The argument, which is a little old-fashioned, has a few flaws in it. For example, recent research on the nature of Elizabethan play-goers has suggested that we may need to revise our preconceptions about the people who comprised the audiences in Marlowe's and Shakespeare's theatres, and about the nature of their 'tastes'. Moreover, as an evaluation of the farcical scenes in Act IV, it has long been challenged by an alternative reading, one which argues that the descent of the action from heroic drama into low farce mirrors Faustus's own descent from an aspiring, 'mighty God' into a foolish prankster. The action, according to this line of argument, is trivial because Faustus himself is becoming trivial. He has gained nothing from his contract with the Devil, and his great ambitions add up to little more than the ability to impress a few fools more gullible than himself. It is not, incidentally, necessary to insist on Marlowe's authorship of these scenes in order to argue that they contribute something important to the play. Whoever wrote these farcical scenes understood well enough the architectonics of play-making, and the serio-comic traditions of the morality plays which lie behind so much of *Doctor Faustus*. This line of argument, then, insists on the overall structural unity of the play.

I would like to make the following suggestions. Firstly, that the argument that the action mirrors Faustus's own debasement is to a large extent correct, but that it is not the whole story. In the first place, Faustus's ambitions, even at the start of the play, were not unalloyedly noble. Moreover, as I hope to show, the audience's relationship with Faustus in Act IV is a more complex business than merely looking down at him with contempt at his triviality.

My second suggestion it that those earlier critics, who emphasized the disunity of the play, and saw the farcical scenes as displaying some sort of break from the more lofty action of the rest of the play, were not entirely wrong. Things in this part of *Doctor Faustus* do operate in a different way from elsewhere, and even if we accept that there is the thematic relevance of the trivialization of Faustus's powers, we are still left with the feeling that the 'texture' of the play is different here from what it is at the beginning and at the very end. I would not, however, make the next step which many of them make when they go on to dismiss these scenes as flaws in an otherwise great play. On the contrary, I would suggest that they contribute to the overall effect of *Doctor Faustus* in three important ways. The first we have already looked at briefly: they show Faustus in a particular light, which helps us in our final evaluation of him. The second contribution concerns the theatricality of *Doctor Faustus*.

In terms of dramatic action, these scenes present an important structural contrast with the beginning and the end of the play. Much of the power of *Doctor Faustus* comes from scenes which are essentially static in nature. (This is not a condemnation of them, but an observation.) We remember how long it took at the beginning of the play before we were presented with dramatic dialogue; even Valdes and Cornelius, when they spoke, tended to do so in large, un-conversational speeches. For much of the early part of the play there are rarely more than three characters on stage at a time, and usually it is just Faustus and Mephostophilis. Inserted into this are occasional larger set-pieces, such as the pageant of the Seven Deadly Sins, but the action tends to be episodic, relying on thematic repetition and parodic balance for its progression. There is little fluidity of action, few connections are made between various characters, since all the focus is on Faustus. He is the only (human) character who seems to have any 'through line': even the clowns, who have a story-line of their own, seem only to appear in response to an action of Faustus's, usually to provide a parodic version of it. In the Vatican episodes the action becomes a little more involved, as the story of Faustus's tricking of the Pope is told. In Act IV, we experience something like a complex plot, as different lines of action intertwine, play across each other, and as characters appear and re-appear in various scenes. It is part of the nature of farce that it has a complicated story-line, and in this section of the play we are given a fluidity of action which was missing in Acts I and II, and only half-present in Act III. By complicating the action, these scenes restore to the play an element of tension – on a very basic level, the pleasure of an audience wondering 'What will happen next?' – which is comparatively unimportant in the main plot, where the audience *knows* (because it has been told by the Chorus, and because conventional wisdom informs it) what will happen next.

The third contribution which these scenes make to the play as a whole concerns the notion of thematic unity again. These scenes comment on Faustus, not just by showing him as a trivializer, but also on another level. The interpretation of Act IV which sees it as merely low farce inserted to please the groundlings, misses out something important: for this part of the play operates in terms of a series of images which, far from being unsophisticated and slapstick, have behind them a strong literary tradition. These scenes present difficulties for a modern reader, not because they are crudely written and without literary interest, but because they adopt a technique of allusion and literary reference which relates them to the main action in oblique, rather than direct, ways.

The farce

Before I go on to examine these images in detail, it might be helpful to provide a brief résumé of what happens in Act IV, since, as I have suggested, the action here becomes more complex.

The Chorus tells us that Faustus's fame has now 'spread forth in every land', and we are to be shown how well this famous man is to be received at the court of the German Emperor himself, Charles V, whom Faustus has already helped by intervening and saving Bruno from the Pope. Act IV, Scene 1, however, emphasizes not the great respect which Faustus commands, but the accompanying cynicism which some show towards him. Frederick and Martino seem impressed by Faustus's reputation, but the inappropriately named Benvolio is utterly sceptical. As Faustus conjures for the Emperor the image of 'Great Alexander and his paramour', Benvolio scoffs from a window above, for which impertinence Faustus sets horns upon his head – the traditional symbol of the cuckold, and the mainstay of a good twenty per cent of humour in the Elizabethan theatre. At the Emperor's entreaty, Faustus removes the horns again, but Benvolio, furious at having been ridiculed, vows revenge. With the unwilling Martino and Frederick and a force of soldiers, he ambushes Faustus, seems to kill him, and cuts off his head. As they gloat over their victory, Faustus comes back to life and sets devils onto them to drag them through woods and briars. When the soldiers attempt to save the hapless gentlemen, they too are driven out by devils. Benvolio and his friends reappear briefly, having been dragged through several hedges backwards, and this time they are all wearing horns. They repair to Benvolio's castle to hide themselves, if necessary for the rest of their lives. The scene shifts to Faustus talking to a horse-dealer (or 'horse-courser'), to whom he sells a horse for the bargain price of forty dollars. Faustus bids him, however, not to ride the horse into water. When the horse-dealer returns, he is furious: disobeying Faustus's injunction, he had ridden the horse into water, and the horse had promptly turned into a bale of hay. The horse-dealer seizes Faustus and pulls off one of his legs, then runs off in terror – upon which Faustus, his leg immediately restored, gets up. At this point, Wagner arrives with an invitation from the Duke of Vanholt, which Faustus accepts. While he travels there, the horse-dealer meets up with Robin and Dick, whom we had last seen being chased offstage by Mephostophilis after the cup-stealing episode. They and a carter (whose cartload of hay had been eaten by Faustus!) compare their situations, and decide to seek out the doctor – presumably to demand recompense or to wreak revenge. The climax to this farcical sequence seems to take place in an alehouse, where Faustus arrives with the Duke and Duchess of Vanholt. The Duchess, who is pregnant, has a craving for grapes, which Faustus has Mephostophilis provide, and at this point they are interrupted by Robin, Dick, the carter and the horse-dealer, who demand something to drink. Faustus seems to comply, but when they start to question him about his 'missing' leg, they find out that he is still bipedal. As if bored with the routine, Faustus charms them all dumb and they exit, leaving the Duke and Duchess well pleased with the sport.

Having sketched out the action, let us now examine the images which that action generates.

The images of farce
(Act IV, Scene 2)

Act IV, Scene 2, in the court of the German Emperor, contains two notable stage images. The first, that of the vision of Alexander and Darius, is significant chiefly for what happens at the end of it. Alexander and his paramour '*salute the* EMPEROR, *who leaving his state, offers to embrace them, which* FAUSTUS *seeing, suddenly stays him.*' Then Faustus says:

> My gracious lord, you do forget yourself;
> These are but shadows, not substantial.

Once more, we are presented with an image of someone mistaking the picture for the reality. As his subsequent conversation with Faustus shows, the Emperor may look but not touch; nor, as Faustus has commanded, may he ask questions or communicate with the 'shadows' in any way. Faustus's admonition to the Emperor seems strange – more urgent than a mere warning that he might be disappointed or unable to touch them. The Emperor's attempt to embrace the spirits carries, it seems, some danger in it, of which Faustus is aware. If this is so, then Faustus's own recklessness is made all the clearer in his own later embracing of the spirit of Helen of Troy.

But Marlowe is also diverting attention, momentarily, from a more important illusion which is being set up while the show of Alexander and Darius is going on. The sceptical Benvolio has had his own prophecy carried out upon him. 'And thou bring Alexander and his paramour before the Emperor, I'll be Actaeon and turn my self to a stag', he had said. And so it happens, for Faustus's magic has set horns upon him.

But why? The usual joke of the horns in Elizabethan drama indicated cuckoldry, but there is no suggestion that Benvolio has actually *been* cuckolded. Why, then, the horns and the references to Actaeon, when, say, an ass's head would have done as well or better? There is something over-elaborate here, and we might suspect that there is more going on than just the practical joke.

In Greek mythology, we remember, Actaeon became so infatuated with the goddess Diana that he desired to catch a glimpse of her bathing, and, although he knew that such a glimpse was forbidden, he managed to do so. But Diana, realizing that she had been seen, turned Actaeon into a stag, and he was hunted down and torn apart by his own hounds. A story, then, of a man who lusted after something forbidden, and who, attaining it, was destroyed by it. Yes, perhaps there *is* something more here than just a joke about a man wearing antlers.

In this scene, Benvolio and the Emperor, in their different ways, both act as symbols and analogies of Faustus himself. Benvolio is a man meddling in something which he does not understand, who gets transformed into an image of a man who found out too much. And the

Emperor foreshadows Faustus's own desire for physical contact with one of his own apparitions when he conjures up Helen of Troy.

A farcical fugue
(Act IV, Scenes 3–7)

Act IV, Scenes 3, 4, 5, 6 and 7 seem to me to make up a kind of farcical fugue, the themes of which (scepticism, revenge and low-comedy trickery) have already been stated in Act IV, Scene 2. The stage illusions of the 'beheaded' Faustus and the repeated and amplified joke of the horns are not without importance; nor is the horse-courser's episode, with its strange amalgam of coney-catching story and folk-tale. The essential joke of this whole section of the play concerns dismemberment. Faustus loses first his head, and then his leg; and then the incident of the leg, which we have already seen once on stage, is told again by the horse-courser and then talked about in Act IV, Scene 7.

This repeated theme of dismemberment seems to have two main effects: firstly it shows Faustus as being less and less identified with his body (he tells Benvolio and Frederick that whatever harm they had done to his physical body he would have put it together again) and thus seen more and more as a spirit. Secondly, it foreshadows the final image of Faustus's limbs, 'All torn asunder by the hand of death' in Act V, Scene 3. What happens here as part of Faustus's practical joking, will happen later as his final destiny.

But the strangest thing about this section of the play is its *tone*. Shakespeare, who is so often cited as a playwright who could appeal to all the tastes of a very mixed audience, never wrote such sustained farce. Moreover, the literate, punning clowns of Shakespeare's plays derive their energy from a totally different source. In *Doctor Faustus*, the farcical scenes are ones which play upon an audience's almost savage delight in watching pride go before a fall, in seeing the best-laid plans of mice and men going painfully agley, at watching the cunning man tripped up (for horse-coursers had about the same reputation for honesty in the sixteenth century as used-car dealers do today), and generally seeing other people punished and humiliated. It is a humour that has a certain moral element to it – none of the victims are totally undeserving of some sort of punishment – but it is above all a *cruel* humour. And how appropriate for the play about the man who sold his soul to the Devil!

I called this part of the play a fugue – and so it is: a musical pattern of repetition, variation and intertwining of themes. We have seen parodic counterpoint in *Doctor Faustus* before (Wagner's parody of Faustus's devil-summoning; Robin's of Faustus's Pope-baiting) but nothing of this level of complexity. If the main point of these scenes is to show the degradation of Faustus, then the way in which the scenes are put together is intricately organized. The sceptical Benvolio has already been punished once, but as he tries to get the better of Faustus he is punished again, in the same way but more severely. While this punishment is happening offstage (literally, while the actors playing Benvolio, Frederick and Martino tie on their horns) the pattern is repeated on a larger scale but in fast-motion as the soldiers attempt to kill Faustus but are, like Benvolio and company, driven off by devils. The Actaeon image, which refers forward, to Faustus being torn apart by devils at the end of the play, is also implicit in what Benvolio does to Faustus in cutting off his head, and this is then repeated in the scene with the horse-courser. He, like Benvolio, attempts to get the better of Faustus and, like Benvolio, he becomes the victim of an animal transformation – this time with a horse which turns into a 'bottle of hay' – and responds by, once more, dismembering Faustus, who, once more, is untroubled by it. The horse-courser is allowed a scene in which to gloat over his supposed victory over Faustus, just as Benvolio and friends had gloated in Act IV, Scene 3; since, however, he is also talking to other victims of Faustus's magic, the scene also contains structural echoes of Act IV, Scene 4, where Benvolio and his companions lick their wounds. In Act IV, Scene 6, the horse-courser's seemingly needless repetition of action which we have already seen onstage makes more sense when it is seen to balance the carter's story of Faustus eating hay. This is thematically as well as structurally balanced, for it brings full circle the metaphorical changes which have been central to this humour. Benvolio fails to pay Faustus his proper respect and is changed into a half-man, half-beast; the horse-courser, looking for advantage in a bargain, gets a horse that turns to hay; the carter thinks he has bested Faustus in a deal but finds Faustus eating all his hay. The peculiar rhythm of transformation and consumption plays across the imagery of dismemberment and restoration, and the animal transformations, too, are brought full circle by the re-insertion of Robin and Dick into the scene, and the reminder that they, too, had been turned into animals earlier in the play. And as a final element of structural balancing, the fugue begins and ends with an intrusion: just as Benvolio had been a rude interruption into the formality of the Emperor's court, so the horse-courser and company intrude roughly into Faustus's interview with the Duke and Duchess of Vanholt.

If the myth of Diana and Actaeon is in the background of the Benvolio sub-plot, perhaps in the background of the Robin / Dick / horse-courser / carter sub-plot is the legend of Circe, another magician who transformed men into dumb animals. This, certainly, is a legend traditionally associated with the dangers of strong drink, and as these four characters drink more and more, they work themselves up into a state of aggressive bravado which finally takes them into the presence of Faustus and the Duke and Duchess of Vanholt, where they are reduced once more to an animal-like state by being deprived of that supreme human attribute, language. Faustus charms the clown and hostess dumb, and brings to an end a section of the play – a section which is much more intricately organized than is generally recognized. Any kind of comic stage-craft depends greatly on timing – from the individual comic's timing of lines, moves and pauses, through to the greater skill of the organization of whole scenes, acts and plays. Balance, symmetry and repetition are also essential ingredients in the farce, and the complex scenes in Act IV of *Doctor Faustus* have these in plenty.

Moreover, the material which is being organized shows Faustus simultaneously as an invincible, indestructible force, and as a twopenny-halfpenny, coney-catching trickster. The audience is progressively released from moralistic engagement with the destiny of Faustus's soul so that it may share with him the cruel laughter of the practical joker. Here is the paradox: in the so-called 'serious' part of the play the audience, certainly, is invited to feel for Faustus in his desires and to sympathize with him in his downfall – but the poised ironic language of those parts of the play, which ensures that the audience is continually made aware of Faustus's mistakes, also invites us to judge him. It is in the farcical parts of the play, where Faustus is most obviously a charlatan, that we come closest to him. For as the comedy actually happens, we share Faustus's point of view. He plays the practical jokes and produces the spectacles for our benefit, and we laugh along with him at the discomfiture of others, from the Pope to the hostess. It is only after the farcical stage action has finished that we step back and make moral judgements on Faustus's share in the action. Before that, we are too closely involved in following the twists and turns of the plot, or in laughing at its outcome. Whoever wrote the fourth act of *Doctor Faustus* was a consummate comedian, who understood not only the traditions of the genre which the play was working in, but also how to manipulate audience response.

A meditative interlude
(Act IV, Scene 5, ll. 21–6)

But Act IV does not contain only slapstick comedy: it also has within it a speech whose positioning is quite extraordinary. If *Doctor Faustus* is essentially a tragic play which has set into it an act consisting almost entirely of low comedy, that act has set into *it* a speech quite out of keeping with the prevailing farcical tone, and totally congruent with the seriousness of Acts I, II and V. In the very short stage-time (less than a minute) between the horse-courser's leaving the stage with his new 'bargain', and his return soaking wet, Faustus, sitting down to rest, has this soliloquy:

> What art thou, Faustus, but a man condemned to die?
> Thy fatal time draws to a final end;
> Despair doth drive distrust into my thoughts.
> Confound these passions with a quiet sleep:
> Tush, Christ did call the thief upon the cross;
> Then rest thee, Faustus, quiet in conceit.

The effect of this speech should be shocking. I suggested just now that our relationship with Faustus in Act IV is different from what it was in Acts I and II, since we are not so closely engaged with his internal thought-processes. This speech, however, temporarily changes all that. Here the dual attitude towards Faustus which I have argued is central to Acts I and II is re-established, as the language once more draws us to him and simultaneously separates us from him. His first question, aching in its awareness of mortality, brings us immediately onto his side – but it should also prompt a series of answers for which the rhetorical tone seems unprepared: he was nothing 'but a man condemned to die' before he signed his soul away to Lucifer; indeed, that was the syllogism which originally turned him to his necromantic books – the disappointment of his discovery that, 'belike, we must sin, and so consequently die'. But now he has a legitimate reason to fear that what he shall die is 'an everlasting death'.

This is not expressed directly in this speech: Faustus is speaking, as usual, with less than total candour. But we are reminded, in the midst of all the foolery, that Faustus's, 'fatal time draws to a final end'. The larger time-scale is not standing still while he sports with clowns; indeed we have a real sense for the first time that Faustus is, literally, wasting time. The speech ends in a way which, elsewhere in the play, might look like Christian orthodoxy, but which here looks like self-delusion. 'Tush,

Christ did call the thief upon the cross; / Then rest thee, Faustus, quiet in conceit.' Faustus says what the Good Angel has said all along, and what the Old Man will continue to say until the day before Faustus's final damnation – that it is never too late to be saved. But although Faustus is right in one sense, he is clearly wrong in spirit. He asserts his faith in Christ's ability to save, even as he is about to immerse himself once more in his cruel farcical stratagems. His momentary 'repentance' turns into an assurance to himself that he can both have his cake and eat it.

We do not, therefore, fully sympathize with Faustus at this point. And yet the pathos of that opening line, 'What art thou, Faustus, but a man condemned to die?', is felt in its fullness because it is positioned in the midst of farce – a farce which seems in retrospect to be not light-hearted, but desperate.

The two Faustuses: the textual problem and Act V

In Act V, the textual problem comes to the fore, and the choices which editors, directors and indeed readers make between the two versions of the end of Faustus's story determine the way in which that story is to be understood. Up to this point we have been presented with the tale of a man whose decisions have led him outside the normal run of humanity. On the one hand we have been invited to see this as a courageous leap of individual daring: Faustus the rebel aspiring to knowledge and power. On the other hand, we have been led to see Faustus as deluded, blind to the fact that, like a character in a morality play, his individuality is not the be-all and end-all of his existence, but that he exists in the larger context of a theological order, which he attempts to ignore but which the audience cannot. 'I think hell's a fable,' is his justification; 'Ay, think so still, till experience change thy mind,' replies conventional wisdom, spoken by Mephostophilis (Act II, Scene 1, lines. 127–8).

According to the expected logic of narrative, the end of the play should provide us with a resolution to this dual perspective on Faustus. In one sense, of course, it does. Hell is not (as Faustus in his heart always knew it was not) a fable, and Faustus pays the expected price for his bravado when he is dragged down to hell for eternity. But the more important question is – how do we react when this happens? Does it happen in such a way as to leave us with a feeling that Faustus is in some way heroic, so that we leave the theatre strong in the sense of Faustus's courage? Or does it happen in such a way as to emphasize the hopelessness, or the foolishness, of his ever having rebelled against the universal order? Where is the imagination of the spectator at the end of the play?

The question is not one of a simple choice of one response or the other. It is a question of emphasis. But it is a question which the text never actually answers for us, for the two versions of the end of *Doctor Faustus* which exist in the original 1604 and 1616 editions tell two different stories. Consider the two following summaries:

1. Faustus, while still conjuring, is harangued by an Old Man, who tells him he is damned. Faustus retaliates by setting Mephostophilis on him, and devotes himself to the love of an apparition of Helen of Troy. Afterwards, seeing his end approaching, he confesses his deeds to some colleagues (the scholars) and then, left alone, in his last soliloquy, he attempts to find some way of escape, but fails and is dragged down to hell. The Chorus reappears to advise the audience to learn from Faustus's fate. (A-TEXT)

2. Faustus, while still conjuring, is offered a last chance of salvation by an Old Man. Faustus, refuses, and retaliates by setting Mephostophilis on him, and devotes himself to the love of an apparition of Helen of Troy. Afterwards, seeing his end approaching, he confesses his deeds to some colleagues (the scholars) – but even as he does so he is watched by Lucifer, Belzebub and Mephostophilis, who have come to claim his soul. He seems not to see them, but finally Mephostophilis appears to him, telling him that he, Mephostophilis, had all along tempted Faustus to damnation. The Good and Bad Angels appear for the last time, now both in agreement that Faustus is damned, and they show him a vision of hell. Faustus is left to his last soliloquy (possibly still watched over by Lucifer and Belzebub) and he attempts to find some way of escape, but fails and is dragged down to hell. The scholars re-enter and find his body torn apart by devils, and they resolve to bury what is left of him. The Chorus reappears to advise the audience to learn from Faustus's fate. (B-TEXT)

Both these versions of the story make perfect sense, but they make different kinds of sense. The one which I put first (from the A-text) leads to a play in which Faustus's tragedy is a private one. We see him alone with his conscience, his fear and his remorse – the individualistic tragic hero. The focus of the last part of the play, right until the moment when hell finally gapes, is unremittingly on Faustus himself.

The version which I put second (from the B-text) places Faustus's predicament in a cosmic setting: the backdrop to his personal tragedy is the whole machinery of heaven and hell. The audience is continually reminded, by the stage presence of the Good and Bad Angels, Lucifer, Belzebub and Mephostophilis, and the heavenly throne and the vision of hell, that the supernatural order against which Faustus has rebelled is real. To put it another way, the A-text shows the play ending predominantly as a tragedy; the B-text has it predominantly as a morality with an unhappy ending.

There is no easy resolution to this duality. If, as I have suggested, we are led to take a dual perspective on Faustus, that dual perspective continues right up to the end of the play. In its earliest printed forms, *Doctor Faustus* quite simply has two significantly different endings. Even when we choose one of those endings to read, to study, to analyse or to perform, we are still aware of the presence of the other in the background.

The Old Man
(Act V, Scene 1, ll. 1–86)

The mood of Act V is set by Wagner's initial announcement that,

> I think my master means to die shortly ...
> And yet, methinks, if that death were near,
> He would not banquet, and carouse, and swill
> Amongst the students, as even now he doth.

The approaching death, and the desperate attempts to forget, ignore or avoid its consequences, are the main themes of this act, an act in which the ethical paraphernalia of the Good and Bad Angels reappear, and are supported on the one hand by the unambiguous Old Man – a 'Good Angel' humanized; and on the other by the extremely ambiguous vision of Helen of Troy. These are the two principal stage images of Act V, Scene 1. Helen is first introduced almost casually, in the same way as the vision of Alexander and Darius. She is conjured up by Faustus and Mephostophilis, she passes over the stage, is admired by the onstage audience, and exits. If anything, it is a less impressive show than the one in the court of Charles V – shorter, less elaborate, with no action to speak of in it. The scholars, clearly, find it admirable, but Faustus himself shows no sign of interest in the appearance other than a conjuror's fondness for his illusion. As a 'miracle', it seems almost commonplace.

It is the appearance of the Old Man which so radically alters the tone of this scene. Up to this point (with the exception of Wagner's ominous introduction) the scene had been a replay of the conjuring of Act IV. The Old Man's entrance pitches the play into a mood of intensity which continues until Faustus's death.

The naturalistic 'background' of the Old Man – who he is, how much he knows, why he approaches Faustus, and so on – are irrelevant. Clearly, he is a functional rather than a psychologically filled-out character. I suggested just now that he is a 'humanized' version of the Good Angel – that is to say, essentially a character whose job it is to present the ethical issues implicit in the plot. Yet the key word is 'humanized'. He is no abstract, no spirit, and cannot be explained away as a projection of Faustus's psyche; he is a creature of flesh and blood, another human being. But in the two versions of the end of the play, the *kinds* of human being that he is differ widely. Here is the Old Man's speech from the A-text.

> Ah, Doctor Faustus, that I might prevail
> To guide thy steps unto the way of life,
> By which sweet path thou may'st attain the goal
> That shall conduct thee to celestial rest.
> Break heart, drop blood, and mingle it with tears,
> Tears falling from repentant heaviness
> Of thy most vile and loathsome filthiness,
> The stench whereof corrupts the inward soul
> With such flagitious crimes of heinous sins,
> As no commiseration may expel,
> But mercy, Faustus, of thy saviour sweet,
> Whose blood alone must wash away thy guilt.

There is an edge of aggressiveness, almost of bullying, in this speech. It begins compassionately, it is true, but soon becomes a tirade against Faustus's misdeeds. Key words are: 'vile and loathsome filthiness', 'stench', 'corrupts', 'flagitious crimes' and 'heinous sins'. Most importantly, the means of repentance are shown here to lie out of the reach of Faustus himself: 'no commiseration may expel' these sins, for repentance itself is no longer enough. The saviour's mercy seems to be offered as a last-ditch possibility, but this Old Man is offering no guarantees that it will be extended.

A central antithesis in the play has been the conflict in Faustus's own mind between the desire for repentance and the forces which drive him onwards in his chosen route to damnation. At this point in the play the conflict is stated once again, but in the version which we have just looked at there is little that is new. Faustus is being given no fresh reasons for repentance, but is hearing the old ones re-stated in a tone which threatens. Given what we know of Faustus's pride, the only surprise is that he listens to this Old Man at all, and does not reject him outright.

I have introduced and analysed this A-text version of the Old Man's speech partly for its own sake, but partly, too, because I believe that it shows up the added dramatic force of the version which most modern editors prefer, the version of the B-text. Here the Old Man speaks a totally different language:

> O gentle Faustus, leave this damned art,
> This magic, that will charm thy soul to hell,
> And quite bereave thee of salvation.
> Though thou hast now offended like a man,
> Do not persever in it like a devil.
> Yet, yet, thou hast an amiable soul,
> If sin by custom grow not into nature:
> Then, Faustus, will repentance come too late,
> Then thou art banished from the sight of heaven;
> No mortal can express the pains of hell.
> It may be this my exhortation
> Seems harsh, and all unpleasant; let it not,
> For, gentle son, I speak it not in wrath,
> Or envy of thee, but in tender love,
> And pity of thy future misery;
> And so have hope, that this my kind rebuke,
> Checking thy body, may amend thy soul.

Here, in the B-text, the function of the Old Man is broadly the same, but the effect of what he says, and of the way in which he says it, is totally different. This Old Man does not speak from the pulpit, but from the ground that Faustus also treads on. Or, to change the metaphor, if the Old Man in the A-text speaks like a judge, the Old Man in the B-text speaks like a friend. The resonances are those of compassion: 'gentle Faustus', 'thou hast offended like a man', 'thou hast an amiable soul'; the threat becomes a warning – even an offer, and it is spoken, 'not,' (as was the exhortation in the A-text) 'in wrath, / Or envy of thee, but in tender love, / And pity'. At no point is this Old Man allowed to bully Faustus – indeed, although his speech is infinitely milder than that of the A-text, he even apologizes lest it seem too harsh.

Why does Marlowe (?) go to such pains at this point to make the Old Man so unlike the preacher of the A-text? As I have suggested, we have no way of proving that either of these versions is more 'correct' or more 'authentic' than the other. And yet I am convinced that this second version is preferable to the first. For it takes into account one of the problems raised by the A-text, and it goes a long way towards solving that problem. The problem with the A-text is that the Old Man speaks so harshly that we are not surprised when Faustus rejects him. The conflict there is baldly stated: Faustus is denounced and threatened, and the opposition is set up between the Old Man, who represents an angry God, and Faustus, who is already so much of a sinner that repentance hardly seems like a viable option to him. Here, however, in the B-text, Faustus is not condemned but cajoled. The element of friendship which permeates the speech in the B-text is something new, and at this point in the play it is extremely powerful. The God which this Old Man represents is not the angry judge, but the sorrowing friend, who is positively eager to extend his grace to Faustus. Perhaps even more important is that the Old Man himself is offering friendship. Throughout the play we have seen Faustus drift further and further into isolation from his fellow-creatures, become less and less of a human being himself. His closest ally throughout has been a demon, his only relationship with any human since Valdes and Cornelius has been that of trickster to victim, or that of showman to audience. The one overwhelming fact about Faustus's situation is its loneliness. And now, by stressing the positive rather than the negative side of Faustus's position, by reminding him that above all he is still a man rather than a devil, the Old Man offers the possibility of Faustus's fully rejoining the human race. Paradoxically, the conflict in Faustus's own mind is intensified because what the Old Man offers is harmony.

What is more, because Faustus is swayed, not by threats of damnation but by the offer of friendship, the audience is more likely to regard him as still being human. The Old Man comes close to succeeding in his objective. Although Faustus's first reaction to what he says is one of despair ('Damned art thou Faustus, damned; despair and die!'), coupled with attempted suicide, thus playing into the hands of Mephostophilis, the Old Man can even dissuade him from this. This is a sign of the Old Man's growing influence – for who else in the play apart from Mephostophilis and Lucifer has had any direct effect on Faustus's actions? For a brief and illusory moment, it looks as though Faustus's fate is genuinely in the balance.

How, then, are we to read the fact that Mephostophilis sways that balance with the most perfunctory of threats, and that the mere fear of physical pain (which Faustus knows lies in store for him anyway in the very near future) pushes Faustus back so securely onto the road to damnation? Are we intended to *notice* the weakness of Mephostophilis's position at this point? If so, we see Faustus here making a glaringly inept decision.

Not only inept, but also vicious. He turns on the Old Man with a naked cruelty which we have not seen before:

> Torment, sweet friend, that base and crooked age,
> That durst dissuade me from thy Lucifer,
> With greatest torment that our hell affords.

'*Our* hell', note. Most critics agree that Act V, Scene 1 sees the final turning-point of Faustus's fortunes, and that hereafter he is damned beyond hope, but I would disagree with those who place the actual moment of damnation at line 99, when he has kissed Helen and thus committed the mortal sin of intercourse with a spirit. That may be the dramatically symbolic moment, but to all intents and purposes the audience sees him as lost when he reveals the capacity for inhumanity which he shows against the Old Man. Ironically, the answer which Mephostophilis gives him reveals simultaneously the danger which Faustus has put himself in, and the pettiness of his own outburst of evil against the Old Man.

> His faith is great, I cannot touch his soul;
> But what I may afflict his body with,
> I will attempt, which is but little worth.

The last five words say it all. As usual, Mephostophilis is more clear-sighted than Faustus about the stakes for which they are playing. As usual, he does not bother to deceive Faustus. As usual, Faustus ignores the truth.

Helen
(Act V, Scene 1, ll. 87–124)

The next image is the most famous in the play, and contains the most famous lines in the play. The reappearance of Helen cues Faustus's big speech. The purpose of her reappearance is significant: Faustus asks for her specifically in order to 'extinguish clear / Those thoughts that do dissuade me from my vow ... to Lucifer'. It is an almost automatic reaction on Faustus's part by now: when troublesome thoughts of repentance afflict him, he seeks diversion.

There is, of course, no doubt as to what 'Helen' is: she is an illusion, prepared by hell, as were the masque of Alexander and Darius, and the parade of the Seven Deadly Sins. Faustus's own warning to the Emperor not to touch beings of the spirit world should here apply to Faustus himself. When she had appeared before, Faustus had cautioned the scholars, 'Be silent . . . for danger is in words'. The warning could almost serve as an epigraph for the whole play. And here, it is the words which Faustus speaks that send the pulse racing again.

Marlowe's sheer skill in putting together moments on stage is nowhere more evident than in this scene. Wagner's earlier intimations of death were balanced by the 'belly-cheer' at which we see Faustus; it was the scholars, not Faustus himself, who first suggested the conjuring of Helen – Faustus had seemed almost indifferent. But there was something about her which caught his imagination, and which now leads him to request her, not just as metaphor but as actuality, not just as vision but as tangible, bedable paramour, and which elicits from him a speech of rapturous beauty. And across all this plays the figure of the Old Man, offering until the last moment a final chance of salvation.

The vision of erotic beauty upon which Faustus fixes, and the language which he speaks, are both doom-laden. Helen is beauty, but beauty which carries with it destruction – the thousand ships are ships of war, and the 'topless towers of Ilium' burnt because of her. Appropriately, the images which Faustus lights upon to praise her beauty and to fantasize about their courtship are also images of destruction: the sacking of Wittenberg, the killing of Achilles, the consuming of Semele by the brightness of Jupiter. But perhaps the most destructive image in Faustus's speech is the one in which, once again, metaphor collapses into literalism:

> Sweet Helen, make me immortal with a kiss.
> Her lips suck forth my soul, see where it flies!
> Come Helen, come, give me my soul again.

Is Faustus not yet aware that the one thing Helen will *not* do is give him his soul again, that it has been 'sucked forth' forever, and that she has no immortality to offer, but only an eternity of torment? Faustus summons the magic of language in order to blot out thoughts of his peril, but the audience witnesses those ideas returning through the language itself.

Once more we should think in terms of different versions of this scene. Act V, Scene 1 might end with Faustus's big speech, and in the original B-text it does so. This gives the scene as a whole three main sections: in section one, Faustus first indifferently conjures up Helen; in part two, the Old Man tries and fails to persuade Faustus to repent; in part three, Faustus turns again to Helen and, swept away by his own rhetoric, he exits with her and the scene ends. But what if one adds another element? In the A-text (which here, unusually, contains a significant detail which the B-text does not) there is a fourth section to the scene. Faustus does not woo Helen in solitude, for halfway through his speech the Old Man enters and (presumably) watches them. And after Faustus and Helen go off, we see the Old Man realize that he has truly failed, and we watch, on stage, the beginnings of the torments which Faustus has arranged for him. What does the reappearance of the Old Man do to this scene?

It is not what the Old Man says that is important. (Remember, this is the rather preachy Old Man of the A-text, and his speech here is in character with his previous appearance.) His very presence, however, changes the way an audience reacts to the whole scene. At the height of Faustus's poetic soaring we are given another perspective on him once again, and reminded that he has given up his final chance of salvation. The presence of the Old Man provides an ironic counterpoint which prevents us from immersing ourselves in the intoxicating eroticism of Faustus's rhetoric. Thus, even if the sub-text of the violent images are missed by an audience, the figure of the Old Man is there to provide a sense of detachment, and to ensure that the audience does not see things through Faustus's eyes alone. And as we watch the beginnings of the Old Man's torture by the devils, and see the physical effect of Faustus's curse, it becomes impossible to ignore the fact that Faustus's sensual ecstasy is founded upon an act of cruelty.

The infernal conclave
(Act V, Scene 2, ll. 1–24)

In my analysis of Act V, Scene 1 I have been concerned to argue that if more weight is given to the figure of the Old Man – first by showing him sympathetically, as the B-text does, and then by having him reappear at the end of the scene, as the A-text does – then Faustus's own situation becomes more complex. He is rejecting an offer which is shown to be attractive, and we see the results of his rejection of the offer. Similarly, in Act V, Scene 2, if we include, as most modern editors do, the appearance of Lucifer, Belzebub, Mephostophilis and the Good and Bad Angels on the stage, we have a play in which Faustus's private, individual tragedy is framed by the cosmic perspective of the powers of heaven and hell.

Some readers believe that this weakens Faustus's own position, reducing him to the level of a puppet, manipulated by external powers. I do not think this is the case. The more sympathetic we feel to the Old Man, the more devastating is Faustus's rejection of him. Equally, the more we are aware of the supernatural forces which are at work, the more powerful is the voice of the individual caught up with those forces.

In Faustus's final soliloquy, the psychology of despair is about to be explored and expressed as never before upon the English stage. The tensions which exist between the speaking voice of the individual and the visual representations of heaven and hell will epitomize the tensions between the morality play of the popular theatre and the emergent individualistic tragedy. Faustus's last soliloquy is a brilliant expression of the isolation of the individual; but it makes its greatest impact when played against the stylistically (and ideologically) very different morality-play elements in the scene. It makes sense, too, that just as Faustus becomes most aware of the reality of his plight, the play should be reincorporating into its overall effect precisely those elements of old-style morality play which most clearly symbolize in theatrical terms the absolutism of the cosmic structures by which Faustus is about to be damned.

Consequently, Act V, Scene 2 begins, in the B-text, with a reminder of the very real presence of the powers of hell. Lucifer, Mephostophilis and Belzebub enter above. Mephostophilis's knowledge of how Faustus's mind works is chillingly expressed as he describes Faustus's present thoughts:

> his labouring brain
> Begets a world of idle fantasies,
> To overreach the devil; but all in vain.

The infernal conclave of the powers of hell usurps the role of Chorus for this final part of Faustus's story, telling the audience, with great precision, what is about to happen.

The scholars and Faustus
(Act V, Scene 2, ll. 25–84)

This exchange between Faustus and the scholars is notable mainly for two things, both of them incidental moments. As Faustus tells them of his plight, much of the scene is a recapitulation of what the audience already knows. The conversation turns into a version of the dialogues of the Good and Bad Angels, with Faustus taking on the role of Bad Angel, and arguing that his position is irreversible, while the scholars urge repentance. This pattern though, lasts only until the scholars are in possession of all the facts. Once they know of Faustus's contract with the Devil, they fall into despair and generally seem to agree with Faustus's assessment of his position. The dramatic tension about whether it is still possible for Faustus to repent seems to have relaxed. When the

Good and Bad Angels appear later in the scene, we will see that it has been dispelled entirely.

In Faustus's exchange with the scholars, Marlowe yet again plays with the relationship between metaphors and literal meanings. Upon being told of Faustus's contract with the Devil, the scholars chorus, 'God forbid!', to which Faustus responds, 'God forbade it indeed, but Faustus hath done it.' The scholars' conventional exclamation is picked up by Faustus and restored to its original force.

In talking about tragedies, it is common to speak about the tragic hero's growth in knowledge, especially in self-knowledge. Such talk often seems inappropriate to *Doctor Faustus*, since Faustus's own growth in knowledge is not towards self-knowledge so much as towards knowledge of what is apart from the self – that is to say towards an awareness of the larger patterns which govern the cosmos: the conventional patterns of orthodox Christianity. He grows in the knowledge of what none of the audience were ever supposed to have been in doubt about in the first place. If one of the tensions in the play as a whole is that between the tragedy and the morality play, Faustus comes to realize, as the play progresses, that his own individual sense of reality is insufficient, and that he is subject to the larger laws of the universe in the same way as every other man and woman. He moves, in effect, from being a character who thinks he is in a tragedy to one who discovers that he is in a morality play.

At this point, however, Faustus does, at least, know what he should have known all along, and one of the ways in which it shows is in his new responsiveness to levels of meaning in language. Faustus picks up both senses of the scholars' exclamation. He takes it on the level at which they originally meant it – as an exclamation of horror – and then expands its meaning to the crucial literal level, which carries so much more meaning for his own situation. Faustus, too late, has grown witty.

A touching moment occurs in the conversation with the scholars, one which is reminiscent of the intervention of the Old Man. One of the scholars offers to stay with Faustus throughout the night. Once more the offer of human companionship is extended. It is a sign of Marlowe's tact as a dramatist that when it is rejected, it is not, at first, Faustus who rejects it, nor is he given the chance to accept it, for the more cautious first scholar dissuades his companion.

Mephostophilis and Faustus
(Act V, Scene 2, ll. 85–96)

The exchange between Faustus and Mephostophilis poses a basic problem of interpretation. Mephostophilis comes down to join Faustus on the main stage, and when Faustus turns on him and accuses him – ''twas thy temptation, / Hath robbed me of eternal happiness' – Mephostophilis gladly concurs:

> I do confess it, Faustus, and rejoice:
> 'Twas I that, when thou wert i'the way to heaven,
> Damned up thy passage; when thou took'st the book,
> To view the Scriptures, then I turned the leaves
> And led thine eye.

This crucial passage once more opens up the dual nature of the play: is *Doctor Faustus* about a man who is tricked into damnation by the agents of the Devil – 'manipulated like a puppet', as one critic has described him? Or is it a play about a man whose responsibility for his downfall lies solely with himself? If we think the former is true, then Mephostophilis's lines here present no problems; they simply reinforce the interpretation that Faustus has all along been controlled by Mephostophilis, and that there was little he could do about it. If, on the other hand, we think of Faustus as essentially responsible for his own damnation, then we might not want to allow Mephostophilis as much of the credit as he claims here.

We should remember that this is a moment in a dramatic dialogue, and that what characters say is, in part at least, always a function of their position in the action. Faustus is in despair and is looking for someone to blame. Rather than blame himself, he chooses Mephostophilis. Mephostophilis, on the other hand, is (from his point of view) nearing the end of a job well done. It is not unnatural that he should be quite happy to claim whatever credit is offered him. It would, I think, be a mistake to read Mephostophilis's statement as a total representation of the truth. For he seems to suggest here that he was continually deceiving Faustus, but we know that this was not so. Certainly, he bullied him from time to time, threatened him, and found devices to distract him. However, he rarely lied to him. Indeed, we have seen Mephostophilis being astonishingly honest with Faustus – assuring him of the reality of hell and telling him about his own torments, for instance. Mephostophilis, in short, has played for the most part the role of the honest servant, only occasionally resorting to bullying and hardly ever to lying or deceiving.

There is, however, another way of reading Mephostophilis's lines – a way which once more involves a shift between the metaphorical level and the literal. If Mephostophilis's words are seen to refer specifically to certain particular incidents in the play, rather than being a metaphor for his general responsibility in bringing Faustus to damnation, they make much more sense. For instance, the 'leaves' which Mephostophilis says he turned may be the leaves of Jerome's Bible, which Faustus was reading in his first soliloquy; thus Mephostophilis becomes responsible for Faustus's original syllogism on the reward of sin being death. Again, Mephostophilis's claim that, 'when thou wert i'the way to heaven / [I] Damned up thy passage', might refer to the ways in which Mephostophilis diverted Faustus's mind from thoughts of repentance with the show of devils in Act II, Scene 1.

Mephostophilis can be seen either as the ultimate cause of Faustus's damnation, or as essentially irrelevant to it, or – as I would suggest here – as being a contributor to it, the agent who intervenes at crucial moments to guide a course which Faustus has already chosen. The ambiguity about Faustus's position remains intact: his own responsibility remains great, but nonetheless throughout the play we have seen him acted upon not only by the forces of hell, but also by those of heaven. An orthodox reading of the play would insist that the powers of hell prevailed, not because they are inherently more powerful, but because Faustus allowed them to do so.

The Good and Bad Angels
(Act V, Scene 2, ll. 97–130)

This final appearance of the Good and Bad Angels shows them in a different light from any of their earlier appearances. Previously, they had been in opposition to each other, now they are in agreement – virtually in harmony, for the Bad Angel completes the rhymes and lines of the Good Angel's speeches:

GOOD ANGEL: O Faustus, if thou hadst given ear to me,
              Innumerable joys had followed thee.
              But thou didst love the world.

BAD ANGEL: Gave ear to me,
              And now must taste hell's pains perpetually.

GOOD ANGEL: O what will all thy riches, pleasures, pomps,
Avail thee now?

BAD ANGEL: Nothing but vex thee more,
To want in hell, that had on earth such store.

And in a stage-picture which describes precisely Faustus's predicament, the Good Angel exits, leaving the Bad Angel alone with Faustus for the first and only time in the play, to gloat over Faustus's damnation and to paint a horrific picture of the tortures awaiting Faustus. '*Hell is discovered*', says the stage-direction, and the audience sees the fate which awaits Faustus. Images of hell cut both ways in *Doctor Faustus*, for we remember that, earlier on, Mephostophilis had contemptuously dismissed the old pictorial notion of hell as a place in favour of a more internalized, psychological idea of hell – 'Why this is hell, nor am I out of it', he told Faustus. Now, however, the audience sees hell as a place, represented on (or below) the stage, and the Bad Angel's description of the place is couched in the old-fashioned pictorial way, as a locality in which,

> There are the furies tossing damned souls
> On burning forks; there bodies boil in lead;
> There are live quarters broiling on the coals
> That ne'er can die; this ever-burning chair
> Is for o'er-tortured souls to rest them in.

All the familiar pictures of hell are there. But just as important are the hints of the hell which Faustus and the audience cannot see:

> But yet all these are nothing: thou shalt see
> Ten thousand tortures that more horrid be.

The picture which the Bad Angel paints is both reality and metaphor. Hell is both that locality with its physical tortures, and also the state of damnation which Mephostophilis understands so well.

Faustus's last soliloquy
(Act V, Scene 2, ll. 131–88)

The exit of the Bad Angel leaves Faustus alone on the stage for his final soliloquy. This speech echoes in structure his first soliloquy in Act I,

Scene 1: once again he is considering a series of options and system-atically rejecting them. The difference is, however, that now Faustus is not contemplating a career for life, but looking for ways to escape an everlasting death. And if the tone of that first soliloquy was one of rational debate, the tone of this is one of utter desperation. The structural similarity, though, between Faustus's first speech and his last, invites an audience to remember that first step which Faustus took, two stage hours or twenty-four fictional years ago, the step which eventually led him to where he is now.

It is a brilliant speech, and one which dramatizes the panic of a terrified mind superbly. No dramatist of the period (except possibly – but only possibly – Shakespeare) had even approached this intensity of stage presence before 1592. The 'one bare hour' which remains of Faustus's life is compressed into fifty-eight lines of text. Yet once again it is a speech which works on more than one level. We are asked to feel more intensely than ever the horror of Faustus's situation – and yet there is that continual irony at work which serves also to detach us from him.

His first stratagem, for example, is to attempt to command the universe to cease its motion. 'Stand still, you ever-moving spheres of heaven,' he cries, 'That time may cease, and midnight never come.' It is not just the pathos of the once-powerful conjuror, still issuing orders to the universe and trying a magic which we know will fail him, that affects us here. There is something unreal about the very command. It is an attempt to escape eternity by compressing it into the eternal moment of the present. He compounds the unreality by asking for the sun to rise again (it is eleven o'clock at night, we remember) so that time will reverse itself, and *then* stand still, as 'Perpetual day'. It is as if he imagines his own life continuing, but the rest of the universe frozen in time. As his end nears, he detaches himself further and further from the natural processes which govern the universe.

Faustus is, in a very real sense, in a world of his own. He would like that world to be one in which his own psychological sense of time is extended, whereas that of the rest of the universe (including the Devil) is either frozen or, failing that, contracted, so that what is experienced by everything else as an hour, becomes to him 'A year, a month, a week, a natural day'. But what the verse enacts is the very opposite of what Faustus is consciously praying for. Even as he asks for it to be extended, we hear time contracting – 'A year, a month, a week, a natural day'. The span diminishes even as he talks.

Moreover, the stage effects contribute to this. The whole speech covers a period of fictional time which is meant to last for one hour. But the speech takes only a few minutes for an actor to speak. As we hear the clock strike at its beginning, middle and end, we are reminded forcefully of the way in which time is contracting in on Faustus. Even more pointedly, the second half-hour of his speech is noticeably shorter than the first. Like his verse, Marlowe's manipulation of stage-time gives precisely the opposite effect from the one which Faustus desires.

Faustus recognizes quite soon that 'time runs, the clock will strike', and he begins to look for other ways out of his predicament. In lines which echo those from Act II, Scene 1, he talks of flying to God. In the earlier scene, after he had signed the Devil's contract, words appeared on his arm, '*Homo fuge*'. We remember that Faustus's response then was, 'Whither should I fly? / If unto God, he'll throw me down to hell.' Here Faustus does try to fly to God: 'O I'll leap up to my God!' The irony in this part of the speech is powerful. We have seen it agreed on all sides – by the Old Man, the Good and Bad Angels, Mephostophilis and Faustus himself – that Faustus is by now indeed damned. Yet even now we are being teased with the idea of his possible salvation. The attempt is foredoomed, it is true. His attempt to leap to God cannot, we suppose, succeed. Even so, the drama plays itself out, and again the failure is seen to lie in Faustus himself. It is not that he does fly to God, and that God then does throw him down to hell. It is that the leap never actually takes place. It is not God, we are assured, who is withholding his mercy, but Faustus who is unable to ask for it.

The movement of thought here is extremely fast. First of all Faustus asks, 'Who pulls me down?' The question is never answered. Perhaps it is the Devil, perhaps it is Faustus himself. There does seem to be a struggle going on between Faustus and something else, but whether that 'something else' is external or internal is never made clear. It prevents him, none the less, from reaching his pictured vision of Christ. Yet even as he utters that cry of despair,

> See, see where Christ's blood streams in the firmament!
> One drop would save my soul, half a drop . . .

we cannot help wondering whether yet again we are watching a man who is fixated with symbols.

This is one of the most powerful moments in the speech. Trying to call on Christ to save him, Faustus here is clearly being tormented physically by Lucifer: 'Rend not my heart for naming of my Christ;' he cries, and then summons up all his strength and all his determination: 'Yet will I call on him: O spare me . . .' – and at exactly the point where we expect to hear the name of Christ, at the moment when it looks as though Faustus will succeed in asking Christ's mercy, the effort collapses. It turns into 'O spare me *Lucifer*!' – and the cry which was to have been a plea for salvation turns into Faustus begging Lucifer not to hurt him any more. And as that happens, the vision of Christ disappears.

Still answering, or trying to answer, the question, 'Whither should I fly?' Faustus looks now for places to hide from the wrath, not of Lucifer, but of God. The image of the martyred and compassionate Christ whose 'blood streams in the firmament' has been replaced by the image of a wrathful Jehovah, who 'stretcheth out his arm, and bends his ireful brows'. As Faustus's desperation increases, so his imagery tends more and more towards the imagery of dissolution. No longer thinking himself capable of leaping up to God, he desires to stand still and let the mountains fall on him; finding that that does not work, he elects to follow a downwards motion, 'headlong . . . into the earth'; that, too, fails for him, so he asks next to become, 'like a foggy mist', sucked up into the entrails of a cloud so that his soul and body can be separated and the former gain access to heaven. All his attempts to escape are here predicated on the idea of *space* – on the supposition that somewhere there might be some place where Faustus might be safe. As the half-hour strikes, though, and Faustus is reminded of the inexorable progress of the last hour of his life, it is to ideas of time that he returns in his attempt to escape. Against his awareness of the terrible reality of eternity, he attempts to set some kind of limits:

> Let Faustus live in hell a thousand years,
> A hundred thousand, and at last be saved.

But just as, in the early part of his speech, he used language which tried to extend time but which had the effect of contracting it, so here he uses language which attempts to set limits to time, but which ends up by expanding it into infinity: 'a thousand years, / A hundred thousand . . . / O, no end is limited to damned souls!'

And then, repeating the pattern of the previous section of the speech, Faustus's thoughts turn again to dissolution. First he thinks of not having a soul at all; then he imagines a soul which is not, after all, immortal; then he thinks of notions of the transmigration of souls and reincarnation. Note that his logic here is confusing: he is attempting to separate his identity from his soul ('This soul should fly from me . . .'). But the whole point is that in a Christian cosmos, the soul *constitutes* the identity. The divorce which he prays for is impossible. He repeats his plea for his soul to be 'dissolved in elements', as the clock begins to strike midnight:

> O soul, be changed into little water drops
> And fall into the ocean, ne'er be found.

This image of the reintegration of the individual into the cosmos, one which in other religious traditions is a natural one for death, is fixed upon by Faustus as a desperate last measure. Theologically, it may itself be a symbol of despair, because it represents an attempt to seek the total annihilation of the soul.

The speech has been a complex series of explorations of possible theological and philosophical escape routes for Faustus, and it has increased in the complexity of its ideas as it has progressed. The last line of the soliloquy, however, contains one of those astonishing changes of direction which Marlowe is capable of when writing at his most intense. Throughout the play, I have argued, Faustus himself is seen in a dual perspective: we are expected to respond to him sometimes with sympathy, sometimes ironically. For the most part this final speech, though not without ironies of its own, has the overall effect of demanding our sympathy for Faustus. We are shown the pain of a man in the grip of terror and despair, and we are asked to understand that pain, accept it and be moved by it. But as the scene reaches its absolute climax, which is also the climax of the whole play, as the action reaches its most intense moment, with Faustus trapped between the Devil and the fierceness of God's gaze, with ugly hell gaping for him – what does he cry out, with his penultimate breath?

> I'll burn my books.

Throughout the play we have seen Faustus confuse signifier with signified, cause with effect, symbol with thing symbolized. Here, in his last seconds, it happens again. The grimness of the humour at this moment is tremendous: at the very point of damnation, Faustus the scholar is suddenly back at his own starting-point, surrounded by those symbols of knowledge and wisdom, his books. Unable, as ever, to differentiate between the various causes of his damnation, Faustus suddenly grasps hold of the idea that one last thing might save him – burning the books. Whether he means specifically the 'necromantic books' which he originally found so heavenly, or the books which Mephostophilis and Lucifer gave him, or the entire library which ended up by leading him towards the study of black magic, the irony is powerful. The large statement is unmistakable: Faustus the scholar symbolically rejects the pursuit of knowledge. But, on a more local level, the gesture is a futile one: Faustus's damnation is not contained within his books, and to burn them would not make one iota of difference to the fate of his soul. The audience takes leave of Faustus, still caught between sympathy and irony, for his last words as he is dragged away to hell – 'Ah, Mephostophilis' – signify nothing, but are full of pain.

Afterword and epilogue
(Act V, Scene 3)

The scene in which the scholars discover Faustus's 'mangled limbs' is usually dismissed by critics as an unwelcome anti-climax. An anti-climax, of course, it is, but that is inevitable after the massive tension of the previous scene. The scholars' platitudes show the action winding down, and the main effect of the scene is to give a sense of the pathos of the 'due burial' which Faustus's remains will be given. The burial service, with its prayers for the soul, is essentially irrelevant to Faustus.

The Chorus's final speech is perhaps less straightforward. Again, it is often dismissed (apart from its opening two lines) as adding little to the drama; or if it is seen to have a function, that function is often supposed to be that of simply tacking a perfunctory piece of conventional moralizing onto a story whose power is actually far greater than that sort of moralizing can comprehend. There is a certain justice in this last view, and it may well be argued that both the scholars' scene and the Chorus's speech are there mainly to reassure the audience that the play is meant to be a moral one after all.

And yet, I wonder. By the end of *Doctor Faustus* the habit of looking for ironies is strongly ingrained in an audience. Is there any way in which irony may be said to operate in this last speech? It is *so* flat, after the pressure of Act V, Scene 1, that I am tempted to suggest that there is.

> Faustus is gone: regard his hellish fall,
> Whose fiendful fortune may exhort the wise
> Only to wonder at unlawful things:
> Whose deepness doth entice such forward wits,
> To practise more than heavenly power permits.

The first of these lines is so grossly inadequate to the process through which we have seen Faustus pass that it almost urges on the audience some kind of opposition: 'But that's not the whole story!' And when the Chorus comes to draw his moral, he does so very strangely. 'The wise' are not warned off entirely from 'unlawful things' – merely instructed 'only to wonder' at them. The speech, too, seems unfinished: it is very short, and ends with a picture of men who are still enticed by forbidden knowledge. How should we react to these last few lines? Should we take them at face value, or should we be as dissatisfied with the conventional moralistic interpretation of Faustus's story as we so often are with Faustus's own account of himself? The answers to these questions will depend greatly upon what we believe Marlowe to have been doing with the Faustus story all along.

Polemical Epilogue:
Elizabethan Magic, Elizabethan Power

I have, in my analysis of *Doctor Faustus*, made much of Marlowe's uses of metaphor. I have suggested that he continually draws attention to his own ambiguities by foregrounding images which may be read either metaphorically or literally. In what follows, I want to consider these concepts of literalism and metaphor as they relate to ways of looking at the play itself. For *Doctor Faustus* may be seen both literally, as a play about magic and magicians, and metaphorically, as a play which uses ideas about magic in order to talk about and to explore other issues which were important to Elizabethan England.

I

In December 1581, when the seventeen-year-old Christopher Marlowe was still in his first year as an undergraduate at Cambridge, a man named John Dee was busy making some rather special preparations at his house in Mortlake. Dee, who was in his mid-fifties, tall and slender with a 'beard as white as milke', was one of Elizabethan England's foremost intellectuals, scientists and philosophers. He was the author of several books and treatises on mathematics, geography, navigation, astronomy, geometry, philosophy and chemistry; he had been science teacher to the immensely powerful and prestigious Sidney family, and he was the owner of England's greatest library. He held offices at the court of Elizabeth, and was one of the most influential scholars in the kingdom. And on 22 December 1581, Doctor John Dee entered the room which he had begun to call his 'chamber of practice', in which stood a table decorated with occult symbols. On the table was a mirror-like object, the 'shew-stone', into which an assistant would peer; and with the help of this assistant, John Dee, the leading scientist of his day, began to summon spirits.

In the course of these Angelic Conversations, which he continued to hold (in a mixture of English, Latin, Greek and an unintelligible spirit-language) throughout the 1580s both in England and abroad, Dee and his assistant, Edward Kelly, conjured up and talked to a variety of apparitions, most of them good angels, but some of them evil spirits. The record of these conversations, meticulously kept by Dee, and edited and published eighty years later by the rather sceptical scholar Meric Casaubon, is often obscure or even incomprehensible, but from it emerges a picture familiar to audiences and readers of *Doctor Faustus.* A man at the height of his mental powers, renowned for his scholarship and intelligence but desirous to know more about the universe than can be learned by conventional scholarship, interrogates the powers of the spirit world, and receives answers which are sometimes tantalizing and mysterious, and sometimes confirmations of the commonly held ideas of the time. In the following extract, Dee and Kelly are in conversation with the angel Gabriel, another angel called 'Nalvage', and a third, unnamed Angel.

KELLY: There appeareth a great thing like a Globe turning upon two axelltrees . . .

DEE: We beseech you to bound or determine the Countries or Portions of the Earth, by their uttermost Longitudes and Latitudes, or by some other certain manner.

NALVAGE: Our manner is, not as it is of worldlings: we determine not places . . . as those that are Cosmographers do . . .

KELLY: There cometh from Heaven like a Mist, and covereth a great place, about 300 mile long, enclosed with fire. It is on a high ground. There come four rivers out of it . . . In the name of Jesus: Is this the Paradise that Adam was banished out of?

ANGEL: The very same. From hence he was turned out into the world.
(From *A True Relation of Dr Dee his actions with Spirits etc.,* by Meric Casaubon. Entry for Wednesday 23 May 1584.)

In an amusing postscript to this particular evening's conversation, incidentally, Kelly goes off in a huff, declaring the angels to be frauds, since most of their revelations derive from a scholarly work by Cornelius Agrippa. Dee, on the other hand, interprets this as a proof that they are telling the truth, and persuades Kelly back to work. This little argument was almost certainly a masterly double bluff on the part of Kelly, who, modern historians are agreed, was a charlatan and a confidence-trickster who made a fine living out of duping the likes of Dee. By revealing his own actual sources of information, Kelly manoeuvres Dee (who wants to believe in the angels) into defending the truth of Kelly's fraud. Kelly, of course, was a version of the phoney medium, who persuaded Dee that he could interpret messages from the spirit world, and who represented himself as the channel through which the spirits would speak.

But my purpose in juxtaposing the story of Doctor Dee with a study of *Doctor Faustus* is not to ridicule the gullibility of the Elizabethan scholar, but to indicate the conditions which made that gullibility not only possible, but almost inevitable. The strict dividing line between alchemy and chemistry, between astrology and astronomy, between magic and science was the invention of a more recent stage of European civilization. More than a century later, Isaac Newton, who laid the foundations for three centuries of mechanistic physics, was still a believer in astrology and in the findings of alchemists. The advancements of learning which were in progress throughout the sixteenth and early seventeenth centuries were not ones which excluded the idea of supernatural influence on the natural world. For a man like Dee to turn to occultism was not an unlikely event: indeed, much of the history of the natural sciences in this period tells of the struggle which was waged on behalf of the scientist's right to explore the workings of nature without being accused of practising 'more than heavenly power permits'. Dee's own reputation in later years was that of an atheist and a dangerous sorcerer – but his dangerous sorcery was thought to include not only his conversations with angels, but also his mathematical researches. Mathematics, after all, is a method of obtaining conceptual control over the natural world by means of arcane symbols – a kind of magic in itself.

It is not my aim to prove that Marlowe had Dee in mind when writing *Doctor Faustus*. What I do want to establish is that in writing the play, Marlowe was not simply spinning an improbable yarn, or dealing with material which his audience would have been able to classify as outdated or medieval: despite the medieval trappings of the play, and its drawing on a legend which refers to a historical Faust who lived almost a century before Marlowe's play was written, Marlowe is writing about issues which are central to his own time. But while I am suggesting the careers of Faustus and Dee as parallels rather than insisting on Dee as a prototype for Faustus, it is not at all improbable that Marlowe knew of Dee, nor even that the two men were personally acquainted. In both of their lives certain incidents and characters appear which makes some connection between the two men a real possibility. At the centre of a complex web is the name of Walsingham.

Sir Thomas Walsingham was Marlowe's patron and friend; it was at Walsingham's house at Scadbury in Kent that Marlowe was staying immediately before his death in 1593. But behind Thomas Walsingham lurks the more sinister and powerful figure of his cousin, Francis Walsingham, whom Marlowe also knew. It is almost certain that Francis Walsingham made Marlowe's acquaintance while the latter was still at

Cambridge, and that either directly or indirectly he recruited Marlowe then for certain duties which were to be carried out on behalf of Her Majesty's Government. For Francis Walsingham was the head of Elizabeth's intelligence operations, and Marlowe was employed by him as a spy.

This phase of Marlowe's life is better documented than some of his later years. He had received his BA degree in 1584, and by March 1587 he had formally satisfied University requirements for proceeding to an MA. The University, however, refused him permission to proceed to that degree. For Marlowe – who in his early years at Cambridge had seemed a fairly ordinary student, living the kind of life typical of an undergraduate in Elizabethan Cambridge – had adopted strange patterns of behaviour. College accounts show that he had been spending more and more time away from Cambridge, and that on the increasingly infrequent occasions when he was in residence, he seemed to have had an inordinate amount of money to spend. The conclusion to which the University authorities jumped, was that Marlowe had been spending his time in France – more precisely, in Rheims, where a seminary for English Catholics had been founded. This seminary was known as a centre of academic excellence but, in the popular imagination, it was also known as a centre of intrigue, and of plots against the English Protestant state. It attracted many poor English scholars with Catholic sympathies, who would begin their studies at Oxford or Cambridge, and then defect to France for advanced study in what the Church of England (and thus the English government) regarded as sedition. After a period at Rheims, and after taking Catholic orders, they might well be sent back to England as Catholic missionaries, *agents provocateurs* or spies.

This is what the University authorities suspected Marlowe of: he was unable to convince them that his absences were innocent, and they refused to confer his degree. Clearly, though, Cambridge had misunderstood the situation, and received a stern rap on the knuckles from an authority higher than itself. Marlowe had powerful friends, and the University of Cambridge received a letter from no less a body than the Queen's Privy Council:

Whereas it was reported that Christopher Morley was determined to haue gone beyond the seas to Reames and there to remaine, Their Lordships thought good to certefie that he had no such intent, but that in all his actions he had behaued him selfe orderlie and discreetlie wherebie he had done her Majestie good service, & deserued to be rewarded for his faithfull dealinge: Their Lordships request was that the rumor thereof should be allaied by all possible meanes, and that he should be furthered in the degree he was to take this next Commencement:

Because it was not her Majesties pleasure that anie one emploied as he had been in matters touching the benefitt of his Countrie should be defamed by those that are ignorant in th' affaires he went about.

Marlowe, it transpired, had not been employed on activities against the state, but had been employed *by* the state, on government service of an intriguingly unspecified nature. It is likely that he was indeed at Rheims, but as a gatherer of intelligence for the English secret service under Walsingham.

Like Marlowe, Dee had spied for Walsingham before the latter's death in 1590. Since Dee was an honoured guest at foreign courts, it is hardly surprising that the head of the Elizabethan intelligence operation should fix on him as a useful gatherer of information. With Walsingham in common, it is not at all impossible that Marlowe should have known of Dee and his occult researches. Moreover, Dee was also connected with the School of Night, the circle of free-thinkers centred around Sir Walter Raleigh with which Marlowe has often been linked. This might have been another point of contact between the two men.

Dee illuminates *Doctor Faustus* in two ways. Firstly in his relationship to Marlowe himself. Both men moved in the same powerful circles and worked for Walsingham as intelligence operatives – thus 'playing roles' in their own lives. Both men, too, were branded as 'atheists' in their own lifetimes. Marlowe was officially accused of this just before his death, whereas Dee's conversations with angels earned him the popular reputation of a powerful and dangerous necromancer – a reputation which horrified him, for he believed his own researches, though unorthodox, to be innocent.

And secondly, there is the relationship between Dee and Faustus himself – both of them respected scholars who turned to the conjuring of spirits, both of them afterwards frequenters of the courts of Europe, fêted by royalty for their occult understanding. It is from this crucible of power, subterfuge, ritual and cosmic speculation that *Doctor Faustus* emerges.

II

And what emerges is a play about struggle. The struggle of a man attempting to assert his own autonomous identity in the face of a cosmic vision which dooms the very attempt, and the struggle between two ways of thinking about humanity's place in the scheme of things. Historians of ideas used to think of 'The Elizabethan World Picture' (the title of a very influential book by E. M. W. Tillyard) as a unified vision of a hierarchical cosmos, a single set of ideas held by the majority of the population and agreed upon by all but a few renegades – such as 'atheists' and their like! More recent research shows the late sixteenth and early seventeenth centuries more and more as a time of intense struggle, a time in which most of the traditional structures of belief were in the process of collapsing and being challenged by new, and sometimes literally re-volutionary, ideas and institutions. The massive authority of the Catholic church was challenged by Protestant beliefs, which were themselves not one single idea but a whole series of often conflicting creeds. In the scientific sphere, a cosmology which, for thousands of years, had assumed that the earth was the centre of the universe, was first challenged in 1543 by Nicolas Copernicus, and then shaken to its foundations in the early seventeenth century by the discoveries of Galileo and Kepler, which established that the earth orbits the sun, and not vice versa. The political and economic structure of England was under continual stress. Bad harvests, political factioning, threats of foreign domination, land en-closures, the rise of an aggressive new mercantile entrepreneurialism – all these and many other factors made for a complex social fabric, and the great achievement of Elizabeth lay in holding together the potentially volatile Protestant state she had inherited. All these conflicts were not isolated events, but the surfacing of a series of interrelated struggles, which threw up questions about the world, the social order, the cosmo-logical order and mankind's place in it.

Drama may not always reflect directly the pressures of the society which produces it, but those pressures are rarely irrelevant to it. At its most basic level, a play is a public event, performed for an audience which will respond instantly with applause or booing. As such, it is written directly for its immediate public and its meaning is constructed in relation to the beliefs, ideas and concerns of that public. Later gener-ations (such as our own) may stage that play again because it speaks to some of their own concerns as well: *Doctor Faustus* in the late twentieth century, for example, may legitimately be understood as addressing itself to kinds of knowledge which *we* find worrying – such as a knowledge of the workings of the universe which enable us to construct nuclear weapons. But in order to understand how the play first came to be the way it is, we need to think too about its original conditions of production.

For example, *Doctor Faustus* has often been seen as a play about pride – and, of course, in a way, that is what it *is* about. But the sin of pride should be thought of in its historical context, for it was a sin with which the Elizabethans were particularly concerned. At a time of exceptional geographical and social mobility in England, when traditional kinship and class patterns were being seriously disrupted, the sin of pride was a political as well as a theological one. Pride meant not being content with one's own station in life, aspiring to change, and thus to destabilize, the hierarchical order of society. The numerous sermons, homilies, satires and treatises of the period on the subject bear witness to the way in which the sin of pride was used as a stick with which to beat those who were not satisfied with their lot, as a stratagem to keep people in their place and as a bulwark against the very changes which were threatening established order and established authority.

The play has been seen, too, as one which deals with the subjects of acquisitiveness and desire for power. Again, a historical context illuminates the contemporary meanings of such concepts. It directs us to think on the one hand of the ruthless drives for power which characterized the political sub-groups of Elizabeth's court (including groups like Sir Walter Raleigh's). On the other hand it directs attention towards the expansionist acquisitiveness of the world of Elizabethan mercantile capitalism, which was already, like Tamburlaine and like Faustus were, restlessly searching out New Worlds to conquer. When Faustus, In Act I, Scene 1, tells of how he will command his spirit-servants to

> fly to India for gold;
> Ransack the ocean for orient pearl,
> And search all corners of the new-found-world
> For pleasant fruits, and princely delicates,

he is doing little more than putting into poetry the dreams of many of the London merchants who comprised a part of his audience. It might be added that such dreams were made into actuality by men like Raleigh.

The real question is: is Marlowe, in this context, a radical or a conservative? If the Elizabethan world picture is one of expansion and change, and one in which various challenges to received political, scientific, religious and social authority are struggling to be heard, then Faustus, in challenging the supreme authority of God himself, comes to symbolize these challenges. The story shows his challenge coming to nothing – in the end he is damned. But the question as to whether we are to see his ultimate failure as an orthodox statement of the folly of pride, or as a celebration of the transgressive energy which made the rebellion possible in the first place, is still open. Those who believe the play to be ultimately conservative point to the fact of Faustus's eventual punishment and emphasize the orthodoxy of the play's overall structure. Those who believe it to be essentially radical maintain that the life of the play resides in the imaginative and poetic flights of fancy with which Faustus himself is endowed, and argue that the impression made by Faustus's rebellion outweighs the conventional morality inherent in the story.

In my own analysis of the moment-by-moment effect of the play I have tended to stress the ways in which the radical or rebellious impulses in Faustus himself are continually undermined by a series of images and ironies which insist on a conventional Christian orthodoxy. I now want to explain *why* I think this happens.

I would suggest that Marlowe, in dramatizing the story of Faustus, the scholar of humble birth who aspires to become a demi-god, found himself unleashing a whole set of energies which were bubbling under in the England of the 1590s, and which he recognized as dangerous. The ambiguity of the play is thus in part a result of Marlowe's own awareness that his subject-matter *was* dangerous. Before exploring more fully the implications of this, I would like to reiterate a few of the things which we know about Marlowe's life in order to emphasize how important the concept of ambiguity is in understanding his writings.

I suggested earlier in this book that the situation of the theatre in Elizabethan England was an ambiguous one, poised as it was between feudal dependence upon the aristocracy and commercial self-sufficiency, between respectability and criminality. The career of Marlowe himself shows a similar kind of ambiguity. When the University of Cambridge refused to grant him his M A, in the belief that he was about to defect to Rheims, they unwittingly expressed precisely that question which dogged Marlowe for the whole of his life, and which continues to dog his afterlife as an author: where *do* his sympathies lie? He began as a seemingly conventional Elizabethan, apparently bound, after his career at Cambridge, for a career in the Church – to become a part of the ruling culture of Elizabethan England and a spokesman for the Establishment. He veered away from this course, and the circles which he moved in during his life included not only the theatre world, but also the ambiguous power groups (including those of Walsingham, Raleigh and the School of Night) which make the history of Elizabethan and Jacobean court life so fascinating. Often potentially subversive, and often portrayed as such, they were also central to the ruling hierarchy. By the time of Marlowe's death he was effectively an outlaw, branded with the label of 'atheist' which stayed with him for so many years after his death. Either he jumped voluntarily or (as seems more likely) he was pushed into that realm of Elizabethan public life which was not 'authentic': the excluded, the marginal, the 'lunatic fringe'.

My suggestion is that in *Doctor Faustus* Marlowe uses ambiguity as a tool. The ambiguity of the play is one by which Marlowe seeks to control the dangerous possibilities of his rebellious hero within a framework which asserts the truth of orthodox Christianity. In other words, Marlowe *needed* the machinery and the world-view of the morality play in order to offset the potential attractiveness of Faustus's daring, in the first place, to challenge the cherished beliefs of a culture. This kind of ambiguity has nothing to do with ideas like 'poise' or 'balance'; rather it is a deliberate strategy to allow Marlowe to think dangerous thoughts and to say dangerous things without pushing himself further into the realms of the marginal. The insistence upon theological orthodoxy which permeates the play is there *because* the initial premise is so radical. It is, in effect, a personal safety-net for Marlowe. For when a supposed or rumoured atheist writes a play about a man who rejects God, it is not surprising that many people have thought of Faustus as being a version of Marlowe himself – the free-thinker challenging the universe. Twentieth-century criticism has tended to play down the suggestion that Faustus the character can be in any way identified with Marlowe the man, but to me it does not seem at all strange that such an identification has been repeatedly made.

'I think hell's a fable,' says Faustus to Mephostophilis. The government informer Richard Baines, whose note to the Privy Council immediately before Marlowe's death is one of the principal sources of Marlowe's reputation as an atheist, reports Marlowe himself as saying something similar. Among the scandalous beliefs attributed to Marlowe by Baines was the belief that 'the first beginning of Religion was only to keep men in awe'. Baines, the supergrass, is of course hardly to be trusted implicitly. Marlowe's 'atheism' sounds very much like the careful smearing of a paid undercover agent. But the opinion which is here attributed to Marlowe is one which Machiavelli had famously suggested, and Marlowe had certainly read Machiavelli. The belief is a perfectly possible one for Marlowe to have held, or to have speculated about. If Baines is not lying, then ambiguity is indeed necessary for Marlowe.

Necessary, perhaps, in more than one way. Necessary to fend off public retribution, certainly. But perhaps also in order to temper for himself the full implications of his own dangerous thoughts. Perhaps the ambiguity of *Doctor Faustus* is so double-edged because Marlowe's own mind is a divided one. On the one hand he is exploring, through Faustus, the ways in which orthodoxy might be challenged by a man whose belief in himself is stronger than his belief in traditional authority. On the other hand, he seems to be asking, 'But what happens to that man if he turns out to be wrong? If hell is not, after all, a fable, and if the first beginning of religion is not simply to keep men in awe?' Playwrights, it has been said, are in the business of asking, 'what if?' What would happen if you took such-and-such a character and subjected him or her to such-and-such a series of pressures? Behind *Doctor Faustus* lies a series of 'what ifs': 'What if a man, now, in the 1590s, should set himself up against the supreme authority? What if he lost? The first beginning of religion is to keep men in awe – but what if it's not?'

I am arguing, then, that *Doctor Faustus* is not a play which makes statements about the world (such as 'Pride goes before a fall', or, 'Man's glory is his aspiring mind'). Rather, it is a play which sets in conflict the ideas of rebellion and authority, heresy and orthodoxy, the medieval and the modern. Marlowe, whose own life shows him to be both establishment figure and outsider, writes a play in which the energies of rebellion are firmly subsumed by the powers of eternity, and he does so out of a self-censorship born both of genuine doubt and of a survival instinct. The forces which he unleashes in telling the story of Faustus are ones which Marlowe himself recognizes as being potent, touching as they do upon questions of authority which were so politically loaded that they needed to be contained within a framework of unimpeachable orthodoxy.

Perhaps, of course, it was not Marlowe himself who felt the need for such containment. It may have been Bird and Rowley, commissioned in 1604 by Henslowe for the considerable sum of four pounds, who found Marlowe's original unacceptable and who took it upon themselves to rewrite it. But this is unlikely, since few scholars attribute the key passages at the beginning and the end of the play to anyone but Marlowe himself. Tempting though I find the idea that Henslowe commissioned their rewrites because he felt the need to water down the potentially subversive nature of the play, I do not believe it. From the very beginning of the play, the complex ironies by which Faustus's rebellion is circumscribed make it more likely that Marlowe's original script contained all the ambiguity of the later revisions, and that it was Marlowe himself who was attempting to use the traditional structures to defend himself against his own imputed atheism.

In the long run, Marlowe did not succeed in avoiding the public accusation of atheism. He was indeed credited with the belief that 'the first beginning of Religioun was only to keep men in awe', and with other beliefs which Faustus might have expressed. Baines, the government informer, concludes his list of Marlowe's supposed heresies with the following statement:

These things, with many other shall by good & honest witness be aproved to be his opinions and Comon Speeches and that this Marlow doth not only hould them himself but almost into euery Compnay he Cometh he perswades men to Atheism willing them not to be afraid of bugbeares and hobgoblins and utterly scorning both god and his ministers . . .

Baines the informer might be seen as a rudimentary kind of literary critic. He is not interested in arguments about ambiguity, or about how potentially radical thoughts might be offset by irony. For him it is enough to note that Marlowe has scorned God and his ministers. The day after Baines filed his report, Marlowe, still under investigation in a case which threatened to involve several 'great men who in Convenient time shalbe named', died in mysterious circumstances in a Deptford alehouse, before he could give witness.

Appendix One: Further Reading

From the wealth of Marlowe criticism, both old and new, which exists, I have made a drastic selection in order to suggest further avenues of exploration. The editions of *Doctor Faustus* by Roma Gill (1965), John Jump (1962), and Sylvan Barnet (1969), all contain useful introductory material. Readers interested in the textual problems of the play should also consult W. W. Greg's *Marlowe's 'Doctor Faustus' 1604–1616: Parallel Texts* (1950).

An entertaining and well-illustrated biography of Marlowe is *In Search of Christopher Marlowe* by A. D. Wraight and V. F. Stern (1965). Three collections of critical essays which chart some of the basic arguments about *Doctor Faustus* are *Marlowe, A Collection of Critical Essays*, edited by Clifford Leech (1964), *Christopher Marlowe, Mermaid Critical Commentaries*, edited by Brian Morris (1968), and *Marlowe's 'Doctor Faustus'*, edited by John Jump in the Macmillan Casebook Series (1969). More recent analyses of the play may be found in chapters of the following books: Michael Hattaway, *Elizabethan Popular Theatre: Plays in Performance* (1982); Judith Weil, *Christopher Marlowe: Merlin's Prophet* (1977); Jonathan Dollimore, *Radical Tragedy* (1984); and (in an essay which deals with several of Marlowe's works) Stephen Greenblatt, *Renaissance Self-fashioning from More to Shakespeare* (1980). Nigel Alexander's *The Performance of Christopher Marlowe's 'Doctor Faustus'* looks at the play from a performance-based point of view and this essay is published in the *Proceedings of the British Academy*, vol. LVII (1972). More easily available is William Tydeman's book *Doctor Faustus, Text and Performance* (1984), which describes several specific productions of the play.

Appendix Two:
Table of Correspondences between Modern Editions

New Mermaids, (Norton) ed. Gill	Penguin, ed. Steane	Signet, ed. Barnet	Revels, ed. Jump
Prologue	Prologue	Prologue	Prologue
Act I, Scene 1	Act I, Scene 1	Act I, Scene 1	Scene I
Act I, Scene 2	Act I, Scene 2	Act I, Scene 2	Scene II
Act I, Scene 3	Act I, Scene 3	Act I, Scene 3	Scene III
Act I, Scene 4	Act I, Scene 4	Act I, Scene 4	Scene IV
Act II, Scene 1	Act I, Scene 5	Act II, Scene 1	Scene V
Act II, Scene 2	Act II, Scene 1	Act II, Scene 2	Scene VI
Act II, Scene 3	Act II, Scene 2	Act II, Scene 3	Scene VII
Chorus I	Act III, Scene 1	[Act III] Chorus	Chorus I
Act III, Scene 1	Act III, Scene 2	Act III, Scene 1	Scene VIII
Act III, Scene 2	Act III, Scene 3	Act III, Scene 2	Scene IX
Act III, Scene 3	Act III, Scene 4	Act III, Scene 3	Scene X
Chorus II	Act III, Scene 5	[Act IV] Chorus	Chorus II
Act IV, Scene 1	Act IV, Scene 1	Act IV, Scene 1	Scene XI
Act IV, Scene 2	Act IV, Scene 2	Act IV, Scene 2	Scene XII
Act IV, Scene 3	Act IV, Scene 3	Act IV, Scene 3	Scene XIII
Act IV, Scene 4	Act IV, Scene 4	Act IV, Scene 4	Scene XIV
Act IV, Scene 5	Act IV, Scene 5	Act IV, Scene 5	Scene XV
Act IV, Scene 6	Act IV, Scene 6	Act IV, Scene 6	Scene XVI
Act IV, Scene 7	Act IV, Scene 7	Act IV, Scene 7	Scene XVII
Act V, Scene 1	Act V, Scene 1	Act V, Scene 1	Scene XVIII
Act V, Scene 2	Act V, Scene 2	Act V, Scene 2	Scene XIX
Act V, Scene 3	Act V, Scene 3	Act V, Scene 3	Scene XX
Epilogue	Epilogue	Enter Chorus	Epilogue

FOR THE BEST IN PAPERBACKS, LOOK FOR THE

In every corner of the world, on every subject under the sun, Penguin represents quality and variety – the very best in publishing today.

For complete information about books available from Penguin – including Pelicans, Puffins, Peregrines and Penguin Classics – and how to order them, write to us at the appropriate address below. Please note that for copyright reasons the selection of books varies from country to country.

In the United Kingdom: For a complete list of books available from Penguin in the U.K., please write to *Dept E.P., Penguin Books Ltd, Harmondsworth, Middlesex, UB7 0DA*

In the United States: For a complete list of books available from Penguin in the U.S., please write to *Dept BA, Penguin, 299 Murray Hill Parkway, East Rutherford, New Jersey 07073*

In Canada: For a complete list of books available from Penguin in Canada, please write to *Penguin Books Canada Ltd, 2801 John Street, Markham, Ontario L3R 1B4*

In Australia: For a complete list of books available from Penguin in Australia, please write to the *Marketing Department, Penguin Books Australia Ltd, P.O. Box 257, Ringwood, Victoria 3134*

In New Zealand: For a complete list of books available from Penguin in New Zealand, please write to the *Marketing Department, Penguin Books (NZ) Ltd, Private Bag, Takapuna, Auckland 9*

In India: For a complete list of books available from Penguin, please write to *Penguin Overseas Ltd, 706 Eros Apartments, 56 Nehru Place, New Delhi, 110019*

In Holland: For a complete list of books available from Penguin in Holland, please write to *Penguin Books Nederland B.V., Postbus 195, NL–1380AD Weesp, Netherlands*

In Germany: For a complete list of books available from Penguin, please write to *Penguin Books Ltd, Friedrichstrasse 10 – 12, D–6000 Frankfurt Main 1, Federal Republic of Germany*

In Spain: For a complete list of books available from Penguin in Spain, please write to *Longman Penguin España, Calle San Nicolas 15, E–28013 Madrid, Spain*

John Aubrey	**Brief Lives**
Francis Bacon	**The Essays**
James Boswell	**The Life of Johnson**
Sir Thomas Browne	**The Major Works**
John Bunyan	**The Pilgrim's Progress**
Edmund Burke	**Reflections on the Revolution in France**
Thomas de Quincey	**Confessions of an English Opium Eater**
	Recollections of the Lakes and the Lake Poets
Daniel Defoe	**A Journal of the Plague Year**
	Moll Flanders
	Robinson Crusoe
	Roxana
	A Tour Through the Whole Island of Great Britain
Henry Fielding	**Jonathan Wild**
	Joseph Andrews
	The History of Tom Jones
Oliver Goldsmith	**The Vicar of Wakefield**
William Hazlitt	**Selected Writings**
Thomas Hobbes	**Leviathan**
Samuel Johnson/	**A Journey to the Western Islands of**
James Boswell	**Scotland/The Journal of a Tour to the**
	Hebrides
Charles Lamb	**Selected Prose**
Samuel Richardson	**Clarissa**
	Pamela
Adam Smith	**The Wealth of Nations**
Tobias Smollet	**Humphry Clinker**
Richard Steele and	Selections from the **Tatler** and the **Spectator**
Joseph Addison	
Laurence Sterne	**The Life and Opinions of Tristram Shandy,**
	Gentleman
	A Sentimental Journey Through France and Italy
Jonathan Swift	**Gulliver's Travels**
Dorothy and William	**Home at Grasmere**
Wordsworth	

FOR THE BEST IN PAPERBACKS, LOOK FOR THE 🐧

PLAYS IN PENGUIN

Edward Albee   Who's Afraid of Virginia Woolf?

Alan Ayckbourn   The Norman Conquests

Bertolt Brecht   Parables for the Theatre (The Good Woman of Setzuan/The
    Caucasian Chalk Circle)

Anton Chekhov   Plays (The Cherry Orchard/The Three Sisters/Ivanov/The
    Seagull/Uncle Vanya)

Michael Hastings   Tom and Viv

Henrik Ibsen   Hedda Gabler/Pillars of Society/The Wild Duck

Eugène Ionesco   Absurd Drama (Rhinoceros/The Chair/The Lesson)

Ben Jonson   Three Comedies (Volpone/The Alchemist/Bartholomew Fair)

D. H. Lawrence   Three Plays (The Collier's Friday Night/The
    Daughter-in-Law/The Widowing of Mrs Holroyd)

Arthur Miller   Death of a Salesman

John Mortimer   A Voyage Round My Father/What Shall We Tell
    Caroline?/The Dock Brief

J. B. Priestley   Time and the Conways/I Have Been Here Before/An
    Inspector Calls/The Linden Tree

Peter Shaffer   Amadeus

Bernard Shaw   Plays Pleasant (Arms and the Man/Candida/The Man of
    Destiny/You Never Can Tell)

Sophocles   Three Theban Plays (Oedipus the King/Antigone/Oedipus at
    Colonus)

Arnold Wesker   The Wesker Trilogy (Chicken Soup with Barley/Roots/I'm
    Talking about Jerusalem)

Oscar Wilde   Plays (Lady Windermere's Fan/A Woman of No
    Importance/An Ideal Husband/The Importance of Being Earnest/Salome)

Thornton Wilder   Our Town/The Skin of Our Teeth/The Matchmaker

Tennessee Williams   Sweet Bird of Youth/A Streetcar Named Desire/The
    Glass Menagerie

FOR THE BEST IN PAPERBACKS, LOOK FOR THE

PENGUIN MASTERSTUDIES

This comprehensive list, designed to help advanced level and first-year undergraduate studies, includes:

SUBJECTS
Applied Mathematics
Biology
Drama: Text into Performance
Geography
Pure Mathematics

LITERATURE
Dr Faustus
Eugénie Grandet
The Great Gatsby
The Mill on the Floss
A Passage to India
Persuasion
Portrait of a Lady
Tender Is the Night
Vanity Fair
The Waste Land

CHAUCER
The Knight's Tale
The Miller's Tale
The Nun's Priest's Tale
The Pardoner's Tale
The Prologue to The Canterbury
  Tales
A Chaucer Handbook

SHAKESPEARE
Hamlet
King Lear
Measure for Measure
Othello
The Tempest
A Shakespeare Handbook

'Standing somewhere between the literal, word-by-word explication of more usual notes and the abstractions of an academic monograph, the Masterstudies series is an admirable introduction to mainstream literary criticism for A Level students, in particular for those contemplating reading English at university. More than that, it is also a model of what student notes can achieve' – *The Times Literary Supplement*